SEX IS NOT THE PROBLEM (LUST IS)

"Full of wise, practical insight, this book offers help and hope—not just for those who are dealing with sexual lust, but for anyone besieged by temptation or battling besetting sins of any kind."

NANCY LEIGH DeMOSS, AUTHOR AND HOST OF THE
REVIVE OUR HEARTS RADIO PROGRAM

"We cannot waste time playing hide-and-seek with lust and its consequences. Joshua Harris has earned our trust by talking straight and teaching from the Word of God. His wisdom on the true nature of lust will not only inform, but challenge every Christian."

R. ALBERT MOHLER, JR., PRESIDENT,
SOUTHERN BAPTIST THEOLOGICAL SEMINARY

"I am very encouraged that my longtime friend Josh Harris has written a book about lust, speaking about the place where compromise begins—the mind. May God use this book to keep many from allowing their minds to become 'the devil's playground.'"

REBECCA ST. JAMES, SINGER/SONGWRITER

"The main issue with lust is that it hinders us from seeing and savoring the glory of Christ. That hurts us and dishonors Him. So, for your joy and Christ's honor, I commend this book to you. It is realistic, practical, and hope-giving because of uncompromising grace. The pure in heart will see God. If you want that sight, let Josh Harris help you fight."

JOHN PIPER, PASTOR OF
BETHLEHEM BAPTIST CHURCH, MINNEAPOLIS

"I may not have kissed dating goodbye, but *Sex Is Not the Problem (Lust Is)* is one of the most powerful books I've read. Josh writes honestly and transparently, giving practical counsel on fighting lust. This is an absolute must-read for anyone who is serious about living righteously."

<small>JERAMY CLARK, AUTHOR OF *I GAVE DATING A CHANCE*</small>

"Joshua Harris has done it again. You hold in your hand undiluted biblical truth on a vital topic, served up with honesty and humility. I'm not aware of another book quite like it."

<small>C. J. MAHANEY, AUTHOR OF *THE CROSS CENTERED LIFE*</small>

"Wow! This book is guts and grace intertwined. *Sex Is Not the Problem (Lust Is)* is a work of colossal importance for both guys and girls. Our generation is in desperate need of this message."

<small>ERIC AND LESLIE LUDY, AUTHORS OF *WHEN GOD WRITES YOUR LOVE STORY*</small>

"A beautiful blend of grace and truth. My friend Joshua Harris raises high standards of holiness while carefully avoiding legalism. Honest, biblical, and practical—I highly recommend it."

<small>RANDY ALCORN, BESTSELLING AUTHOR OF *THE TREASURE PRINCIPLE* AND *THE PURITY PRINCIPLE*</small>

"Forthright, honest, and compelling. Joshua Harris has written a book about sexual purity that can be read and applied by both men and women. He shows us in practical and specific ways how we can grow toward God's standard—absolute purity in mind and body."

<small>JERRY BRIDGES, AUTHOR OF *THE PURSUIT OF HOLINESS*</small>

SEX IS NOT THE PROBLEM (LUST IS)

JOSHUA HARRIS

Multnomah Books

SEX IS NOT THE PROBLEM (LUST IS)
published by Multnomah Books

© 2003 by Joshua Harris
International Standard Book Number: 978-1-59052-519-7

Cover image by Stephen Gardner, PixelWorksStudio.net
Author photo by Matt Mendelsohn photography

Unless otherwise indicated, Scripture quotations are from:
The Holy Bible, New International Version © 1973, 1984 by International Bible Society,
used by permission of Zondervan Publishing House
Other Scripture quotations are from: The Holy Bible, *English Standard Version* (ESV)
© 2001 by Crossway Bibles, a division of Good News Publishers.
Used by permission. All rights reserved.
The Message
© 1993, 1994, 1995, 1996, 2000, 2001, 2002
Used by permission of NavPress Publishing Group
Holy Bible, New Living Translation (NLT)
© 1996. Used by permission of Tyndale House Publishers, Inc.
All rights reserved.

Published in the United States by WaterBrook Multnomah,
an imprint of the Crown Publishing Group,
a division of Random House Inc., New York.

MULTNOMAH and its mountain colophon are registered trademarks of Random House Inc.

For information:
MULTNOMAH BOOKS
12265 ORACLE BOULEVARD, SUITE 200 • COLORADO SPRINGS, CO 80921

Library of Congress Cataloging-in-Publication Data

Harris, Joshua.
  Sex Is Not the Problem (Lust Is) / by Joshua Harris.
      p. cm.
Includes bibliographical references.
  ISBN 1-59052-519-1
  ISBN 1-59052-147-1
  1. Lust—Religious aspects—Christianity. I. Title.
  BV4627.L8H37 2003
  241'.3—dc21
                        2003010045

11—20 19 18 17

For my children,
Emma Grace
and
Joshua Quinn.

Contents

Preface

When I first told my father-in-law I was writing a book on lust, he humorously asked, "So are you for it or against it?" I laughed and told him that I'm against lust and that I think there's already enough literature in favor of it! But later I realized that the message of this book is not that I'm against lust, but that I'm for God's plan for·sexual desire. Yes, lust is bad. But it's bad because what it perverts is so good.

Some people have the mistaken notion that God is anti-sex. In fact, He's outspokenly pro-sex! He invented it. What an incredible thought! Passionate sex was God's idea.

He isn't embarrassed by it. Song of a Songs is an entire book in the Bible dedicated to celebrating pure sex in marriage.

Part of the challenge Christians face in a lust-filled world is remembering that neither sex nor sexuality is our enemy. Sex is not the problem—lust is the problem. It's the enemy and has hijacked sexuality. We need to keep reminding ourselves that our goal is to rescue our sexuality from lust so we can experience it the way God intended.

That being said, let me be the first to admit that I need this book as much as or more than anyone else who will ever read it. I wrote it not because I've "conquered" lust and have a foolproof plan for you to follow; I wrote it because I've experienced God's power to change, and I know He wants you to experience that power too.

Two years ago, I was preparing to give a message on lust when I realized that the book I wanted to consult hadn't been written. That book would make it clear that only Jesus Christ can free us from the hopeless treadmill of shame and guilt that so many well-intentioned people end up on. It would be a "PG-rated" book that would instill a love for holiness and a hatred for lust without dragging the reader's imagination through the gutter. And it would be for both men and women, because I've learned that lust isn't just a guy problem—it's a human problem.

This is my humble attempt to write that book. And though I'm now happily married, much of what you'll read is directed toward single men and women. That's because so often it's during the single years that lust gains a foothold in a person's life. But the principles in this book aren't limited to singles or to a certain age group. I hope many married people will read it and benefit too.

If you're a Christian, I want to remind you of truths you may have allowed to slip. If you're reading this and you're not a Christian, please don't let my religious terms scare you off. If you're frustrated by the way lust controls and shapes your life and are plagued by guilt, I want to introduce you to the Savior who has forgiven me and changed my life.

I've learned that I can only fight lust in the confidence of my total forgiveness before God because of Jesus' death for me. My guilt and shame, even self-inflicted punishment, can never cleanse me. Even my good works can't buy my forgiveness. I need a Savior. I need grace.

Author Jerry Bridges says it best: "Every day of our Christian experience should be a day of relating to God on the basis of His grace alone," he writes. "Your worst days are never so bad that you are beyond the reach of God's grace. And your best days are never so good that you are beyond the need of God's grace."

Whether you're having a "good day" or "bad day," my prayer is that something in this small book will introduce you to the life you really want—a life more pleasing to God, a life marked by deep inward purity, a life that knows both the pleasure and the freedom of holiness.

JOSHUA HARRIS

Part One

The Truth About Lust

Not Even a Hint

Why Can't I Seem to Beat Lust?

Seven of us were gathered in the dimly lit living room. A single sheet of notebook paper passed slowly between each person. Finally, it came to me. I scanned the numbered list then solemnly signed my name at the bottom of the page.

The "contract," as we had come to call it, was a strict code of conduct, a list of promises that each of us was vowing to follow for the coming year.

We would read our Bibles every day.

Go to church every Sunday.

Memorize a passage of Scripture every week.

Fast every Tuesday.

Share our faith with one person each week.

We wouldn't watch any movies.

We wouldn't kiss a girl.

We wouldn't drink alcohol.

And we wouldn't masturbate.

Actually, I don't remember all the promises on the list. I think there were nearly fifteen. But I distinctly remember that the vow to refrain from masturbating was number ten on the list. That promise held the particular attention of each of us.

The Stallions

I was eighteen years old. The other six guys ranged in age from seventeen to twenty-four. That summer we were working as counselors at a Christian leadership camp in Colorado. Carlos, Clint, and I washed dishes. Don, Brook, Jon, and Scot shuttled students in the vans. We called ourselves "The Stallions"—named after a cabin several of the guys lived in.

I can't remember exactly when the idea for the contract came up. I guess we wanted rules. We wanted to know we were pleasing God. The whole process of becoming holy seemed complicated to us, so the idea of reducing our faith to a manageable list of promises and prohibitions was appealing.

So there we were in Jon's parents' living room signing our names. After we were done, Jon took the piece of paper, placed it on the floor in the center of the room, and knelt beside it. "C'mon, guys," he said. "Let's seal our vow with prayer."

The whole thing was very dramatic. All that was missing was a rising orchestral theme playing in the background. We got down on our knees, huddled in a circle, and extended our right hands onto the sheet of paper. We closed our eyes and bowed our heads, then pledged before God to obey every rule on the list.

It was official. The contract was ratified. I felt sure that the angels in heaven must be leaning down in amazement, watching our impressive display of godliness and the sheer strength of will in the room.

A few days later, we all left for home. I was still basking in the euphoria of our religious zeal. Every generation needs men of courage, men of conviction, men of strength—men of God. I was one of those men.

The illusion lasted about two weeks. That's when I broke rule number ten of the contract.

The year that followed was a very humbling lesson in how utterly incapable I was of being righteous in my own strength. And I wrote "number ten again" in my journal more times that year than I want to think about. All my great ambitions, all my vows, all my self-efforts were revealed to be worthless.

A Defining Struggle

I can laugh now as I look back on that year under the tyranny of "the contract," but it really taught me some important lessons about the limitations of human rules and regulations to bring about real change in a person's life—especially in the area of lust.

Of course, masturbation is just one of the myriad ways that sexual lust manifests itself in our lives. Your struggle with lust might look quite different from mine. It could involve romantic fantasies, Internet pornography, or the temptation to get sexually involved with a boyfriend or girlfriend. Because the possibilities are endless, I have a simple definition for lust: Lust is craving sexually what God has forbidden.

To lust is to want what you don't have and weren't meant to have. Lust goes beyond attraction, an appreciation of beauty, or even a healthy desire for sex—it makes these desires more important than God. Lust wants to go outside God's guidelines to find satisfaction.

I've come to believe that lust may be *the* defining struggle for this generation. Writing two books on the topic of dating and courtship in the last five years has helped me see just how serious this problem is for a broad spectrum of believers. I've received thousands of letters and e-mails from people of all ages around the world who are struggling with sexual impurity.

The stories are heartbreaking, and they're from both women and men. They're stories of small compromises that led to serious sin and regret. They're stories of secret and anguishing battles with premarital sex, with pornography, and with homosexuality. They're stories from those who once swore to remain pure and now can't believe the depths of impurity to which they've descended.

One girl named Chelsea, who found herself trapped in a web of masturbation and Internet pornography, wrote me. Her letter is typical of the desperation and frustration of so many:

> I don't know who I am anymore. I am so scared....
> I do what I know is wrong. I have tried to stop—
> really, I have. I have cried and sobbed at night. I

have prayed and kept journals. I have read books. I am honestly at a loss. I love God, but I cannot continue to ask for forgiveness over and over and over for the same thing. I know I need help, but I don't know how to get it. I know that God has so much more planned for my life than this. But this sin continues to conquer me.

Can you relate to Chelsea's anguish? You try and try, but it never seems to be enough. Is there anything more discouraging than losing the fight against lust? It saps your spiritual passion. It makes your faith feel hollow. It stifles prayer. It colors your whole view of your walk with God. At moments you're so overwhelmed by shame that God seems a million miles away.

WHAT ARE WE DOING WRONG?

Is this how it's supposed to be? Did Jesus die to win *this* for us?

No, it's not. God doesn't want you to live in an endless cycle of defeat. Chelsea is right. Our heavenly Father *does* have so much more planned for us than a life dominated by lust, guilt, and shame. So why don't we experience it? What are we doing wrong?

In our losing battle against lust we're often misguided in three key areas. We've had...

- the wrong *standard* for holiness,
- the wrong *source* of power to change,
- and the wrong *motive* for fighting our sin.

My failure to uphold "the contract" was my first clue that my method for resisting lust was misguided. To begin with, it was based on my own standard of what it meant to obey God. I created a rule I thought I could follow—I wouldn't masturbate for a year.

The result was that I placed my hope in the wrong source of power to obey—my own willpower and strength. I wasn't putting my faith in God; I was putting my faith in Joshua Harris and his ability to resist temptation.

My motivation didn't help either. Though it wasn't completely wrong—part of me genuinely wanted to please God—a huge part of my motivation was to "feel" like a pure person. I wanted to be able to say I hadn't sinned. I wanted to show God how good I could be and how worthy I was.

But of course it all fell apart. After I sinned again, my motivation crumbled. I didn't feel pure or worthy of God's love. My guilt made me reluctant to pray. So I tried harder to muster the willpower to stop lusting. This only led to more discouragement and frustration. Even when I revised my standards—"I won't do it for the next *nine* months!"— the whole cycle repeated itself again.

Can you relate? Do you see how getting our standard, source of power, and motivation all wrong leads to ongoing failure?

I wrote this book because I've learned that I don't have to live on this treadmill. You don't have to either. God's Word shows us how to get on the path to freedom. It shows us that the key to escaping the cycle of defeat is to embrace God's standard for holiness, His source of power for change, and His motive for fighting sin.

DUELING STANDARDS

So what *is* God's standard when it comes to lust? How much lust does God want us to allow in our lives?

Are you ready for this? The answer is *not even a hint.*

That's right. Nada. Zip. Zero.

I'm not saying this to be dramatic. I really believe it's what God calls each Christian to regardless of what kind of culture we live in or how old we are. And it's not because God is heavy-handed, or strict for the sake of strictness. It's because He loves us—and because we are His. It's because

He is wise and His wisdom exceeds our understanding.

Ephesians 5:3 says:

> But among you there must not be even a hint of sexual immorality, or of any kind of impurity, or of greed, because these are improper for God's holy people.

We'll learn more later about why God set His standard so high. But for now, it's enough to note that to acts of "sexual immorality" God adds "or any kind of impurity." It's not just the sins of adultery and sex outside of marriage God wants us to be freed from. He wants us to eliminate any kind of impurity in our thoughts and actions. He wants us to dig down into our hearts and uproot sexual greediness, which is always seeking a new sensual thrill.

But instead of that, a lot of us have developed a diet mentality toward lust. We really want to cut back on lust because we know it's not healthy and it makes us feel bad. But like some rich, calorie-laden chocolate dessert, lust is just too tasty to resist completely. Surely God will understand if we break our diet and nibble a little lust now and then (get too intimate on a date here, watch a questionable movie there, or indulge in an ungodly fantasy).

This is the same kind of thinking behind the age-old question asked in youth groups: "How far is too far?"

Isn't just a little lust okay? You can see how our diet mentality leads us to set up a lower standard than God's. You might call it "A little won't hurt." And, hey, it sounds like a reasonable standard. Best of all, at least on the surface, it seems doable!

There's just one problem: The Bible teaches the opposite. A little lust is not okay. That's why God calls us to the daunting standard of *not even a hint*. This means there's no place for lust to exist peacefully in our lives. We're to fight it on every front.

Sounds exhausting, doesn't it? But if you're feeling like the bar is set hopelessly high, don't give up. That's exactly what you should be feeling....

"But That's Impossible!"

When I was deciding what to call this book, one person suggested *I Kissed Lust Goodbye*. My first book, *I Kissed Dating Goodbye,* had done well, he reasoned, and my new book would benefit from being tied to it. Besides, isn't that what we want to do—kiss lust goodbye?

Well, yes it is, but I didn't like the idea. It made it sound like ridding our lives of lust is an easy thing. As if it's something that everybody, if they're so inclined, can simply decide to do. But if you've tried to turn your back on lust, you know this isn't so. Lust and impurity entice us, ensnare us, and dog us even after we've sworn them off for the thousandth time.

Sexual purity is clearly something only God can bring about in your life and mine. God's standard of *not even a hint* quickly brings me to the end of my own ability and effort. It reminds me that God's standard is so much higher than the standards I place for myself that only the victory of Christ's death and resurrection can provide the *right power* and the *right motive* needed to change me.

Willpower won't work. Only the power of the cross can break the power of sin that keeps us on its treadmill.

Despair or pride that I can change won't work either. Only the motive of grace—trust in the undeserved favor of God—can inspire us to pursue holiness free from fear and shame.

THE PROMISE OF PLEASURE

In *The Great Divorce,* C. S. Lewis tells an allegorical story about a ghost of a man afflicted by lust. Lust is incarnated in the form of a red lizard that sits on his shoulder and whispers seductively in his ear. When the man despairs about the lizard, an angel offers to kill it for him. But the fellow is torn between loving his lust and wanting it to die.

He fears that the death of the lust will kill him. He makes excuse after excuse to the angel, trying to keep the lizard he says he doesn't want. (Are you starting to see yourself?)

Finally, the man agrees to let the angel seize and kill the lizard. The angel grasps the reptile, breaks its neck, and throws it to the ground. Once the spell of lust is broken, the ghostly man is gloriously remade into a real and solid being. And the lizard, rather than dying, is transformed into a breathtaking stallion. Weeping tears of joy and gratitude, the man mounts the horse and they soar into the heavens.

In this story, C. S. Lewis shows the connection between killing our lust and finding life. It feels as though destroying our lust will destroy us. But it doesn't. And when we destroy our lustful desire, we come not to the end of desire, but to the beginning of *pure desire*—God-centered desire, which was created to carry us into the everlasting morning of God's purposes.

God never calls us to sacrifice as an end in itself, but only *through* sacrifice on the way to great joy. On the other side of the seeming loss and denial is always reward and pleasure so deep and so intense that it's almost impossible to call what you gave up a sacrifice at all. And that's true even if the suffering and self-denial God calls us through lasts a lifetime.

If you ever expect to find victory over lust, you must believe with your whole heart that God is against your lust not because He is opposed to pleasure, but because He is so committed to it.

In his book *Future Grace,* John Piper writes:

We must fight fire with fire. The fire of lust's pleasures must be fought with the fire of God's pleasures. If we try to fight the fire of lust with prohibitions and threats alone—even the terrible warnings of Jesus—we will fail. We must fight it with the massive promise of superior happiness. We must swallow up the little flicker of lust's pleasure in the conflagration of holy satisfaction.

Do you want to be free from the oppression of lustful desires and actions? Do you want to get off the treadmill of guilt and shame?

God offers you and me hope in a surprising way. He doesn't tell us to lower our standards to a place where we think we can do it in our own strength. He calls us to embrace the standard of His Word—not even a hint of sexual immorality or impurity. God wants us to despair in our own strength so that we have no other option but to throw ourselves on His grace.

That's the mystery of His plan. You will find His strength in your weakness. As you despair in yourself, you will find hope in Him. And as you turn your back on lust, you will discover that true pleasure is something only God can give.

chapter two

Sex Is Not the Problem

Is It Biology or Is It a Sin?

The phone rings. "Hello?"

"Hey, buddy, it's me. How's it goin'?"

It's my friend Drew. I can tell by the tone of his voice exactly what he's calling to talk about.

"I'm doing fine," I reply. "How are *you?*" I sit down on the couch. It's going to be a long conversation—Drew needs to have a "girl talk."

"Oh, I'm okay," Drew says.

"Sure you are."

"I don't know," he continues. "I'm just such an idiot. I saw her today, and I didn't go talk to her. I just waved at her. I mean, I can't even be myself around her. Why can't I just talk to her and treat her like any other girl?"

"Because you're an idiot," I say with a smile.

"I know that!"

We talk for the next forty minutes about getting up the nerve to talk with a girl you like, about just what it is he finds so attractive about her, and about what it means for them to develop a friendship. Then we walk through, one more time, all he needs to do on the path toward marriage readiness. He's almost done with school. He needs to choose between graphic design and photography. He needs to make sure he can make a living and support a family. I listen to him and I smile. I'm proud of him. He's working, he's straining, he's planning—driven on by a God-planted desire to win a girl's heart.

As I listened to Drew, I remembered myself in the years leading up to my marriage. I thought of all the times I overcame apathy because of the same incessant drive. I was struck by what an awesome, wise thing it was for God to make men and women sexual creatures with a magnetic attraction to each other.

At times, especially when I was single, I've been tempted to view my sex drive as more of a curse than a blessing. But how untrue that is! In fact, it's the very lie

Satan wants us to believe—that our sexuality itself is sinful. He knows that if he can confuse us about the difference between our God-given sexual nature and the corrupting influence of lust, our efforts to battle sin will be sabotaged before we even walk out the door.

Before we can fully grasp why God says there should be *"not...even a hint"* of lust in our lives, we need to understand what lust *is* and what it is not. And before we can attack the lust in our lives with conviction, we need to reclaim sexual desire as God's amazing and good gift to us.

THE GOOD DRIVE

That night, as I listened to Drew and thought about all the ways he was exerting himself because he's a man and because he *wants* a woman—in every godly sense of the word, including sexually—I caught a glimpse of just how *good* it is that God made us like He did.

He really knew what He was doing, didn't He? "Be fruitful and...multiply," he commanded mankind (Genesis 9:7). And then, just in case we'd be tempted to slack off in this task of populating and subduing the earth, He made us sexual creatures and wired us with this incredible thing we call a sex drive.

What is this drive anyway? One day it lands on our

doorstep and life is never the same. One moment you're a kid and the opposite sex is yucky—boys are gross and girls have cooties. The next day the world turns upside down. Hormones begin to pump, your body transforms, hair starts to show up in weird places, and this pulsing, driving, burning sexual awareness and desire begins flowing through your veins like molten lava. Welcome to puberty. Welcome to humanity.

God gave us our drives so we would drive *toward* something. Just as He gave us an appetite for food so that we wouldn't forget to feed our bodies, He gave us a sexual appetite so that men and women would keep being joined together and creating offspring in marriage.

And beyond procreation, our sex drive is in some mysterious way part and parcel of our drive to build, advance, conquer, and survive. Our sexuality and our sex drive are intertwined and tied together with our creativity and with our innate human desire to continue life on this spinning planet. Being a sexual being with sexual desires is part of what it means to be a human created in God's image.

Think about this: The sinless Son of God, who perfectly obeyed God's commands for purity and never lusted, was *completely* human. That means Jesus was a *sexual* human being. God didn't fudge on the Incarnation. God became one of us—a living, breathing, sweating, desiring, feeling human being. Jesus wasn't a sexless, lifeless half-

man. He had sexual urges and desires. He appreciated the
beauty of women. He noticed the beauty of women. He
was really a man...and none of this was sinful.

The truth is that Jesus didn't come to rescue us from
our humanity; He entered into our humanity to rescue us
from our sinfulness. He didn't come to save us from being
sexual creatures; He became one of us to save us from the
reign of sin and lust, which ruins our sexuality.

That's why it's so critical to understand that our sexual
drive isn't the same as lust. For example:

- It's *not* lust to be attracted to someone or notice that
  he or she is good-looking.
- It's *not* lust to have a strong desire to have sex.
- It's *not* lust to anticipate and be excited about having
  sex within marriage.
- It's *not* lust when a man or woman becomes turned-
  on without any conscious decision to do so.
- It's *not* lust to experience sexual temptation.

The crucial issue in each of these examples is how we
respond to the urges and desires of our sexual drive.
Noticing an attractive person is not wrong; but undressing
that person with your eyes or imagining what it would be
like to "have" them is. A sexual thought that pops into your
mind isn't necessarily lust, but it can quickly become lust

if it's entertained and dwelled on. An excitement for sex in marriage isn't sin, but it can be tainted by lust if it's not tempered with patience and restraint.

If you fail to make these distinctions, your fight against lust will be greatly hampered. On the one hand, you can wind up excusing sinful thoughts and actions as "just part of how I'm made," which isn't true at all. On the other, you may end up being ashamed of your sex drive, which God never intended. Both are tragic mistakes.

IT'S A SHAME

When we break God's commands, shame is appropriate. In fact, it can be a precious gift from God. An awareness that we've done wrong—those feelings of conviction and guilt that cause us to feel shame can lead to repentance and restoration.

That being said, it is possible for a person to experience misplaced shame, which results from what you could call a wrongly programmed conscience. Misplaced shame is shame in response to values other than those found in God's Word. If your upbringing, or faulty teaching, or harmful past sexual experience leaves you feeling ashamed of aspects of your sexuality that God doesn't say are sinful, He can help you renew your mind. He can help you bring your attitude about sex in line with His values.

Misplaced shame can be dangerous because it saps our strength for fighting our real enemy. A person who is wrongly ashamed of being a sexual creature with sexual desires will quickly feel overwhelmed and helpless because he's trying to overcome more than just lust—he's trying to stop being human!

One way to get rid of misplaced shame is to talk to God about your sexual feelings. Invite His Spirit into the day by day, moment by moment process of yielding your sexual desire to His will. These are the kind of interactions and prayers I'm talking about:

- *God, thank You for making me a sexual creature with sexual desires! I don't ask that You remove my desire, but that You help me to please You with it in my thoughts and actions.*
- *God, in this moment my whole body seems to be screaming for sexual satisfaction—would You please quiet my desires? My body was made for You and for holiness, not for sexual sin. Help me to glorify You with my body.*
- *God, You made me for true and lasting pleasure! Fill me with confidence that You have good things in store for me—something much better than what lust has to offer.*
- *God, thank You for beauty and for my ability to appreciate it. That person is very attractive. But let me look on*

him with purity. I don't want to covet and lust after him.
Help me to view him as a person made in Your image,
not an object of my lust.

• *God, I'm tempted to look to lust for comfort right now.*
Please help me to find my comfort in You.

Do you see how this kind of open, humble dialogue
with God could transform the way you view your sexuality? Remember, God doesn't just want us to cultivate a
hatred for lust; He wants us to cultivate a gratefulness
and appreciation for the gift of sexual desire He has
planted in us.

THE NATURE OF LUST

The potential for misplaced shame makes it all the more
important to have a clear understanding of what lust really
is and where it comes from.

John Piper explains lust with this simple equation:
"Lust is a sexual desire minus honor and holiness." When
we lust, we take this good thing—sexual desire—and
remove from it honor toward fellow humans and reverence
for God.

Lust is an idolatrous and ultimately insatiable desire
that rejects God's rule and seeks satisfaction apart from

Him. God says, "You shall not covet" (Exodus 20:17). But lust tells us that what we don't have is exactly what we need. *Lust covets the forbidden.* Lust grasps for, with our eyes, hearts, imaginations, or bodies, what God has said no to.

And what is the *source* of our lust? When we sin, it's our own evil desire that entices us. James 1:14 says, "Each one is tempted when, by his own evil desire, he is dragged away and enticed." And Jesus taught, "For out of the heart come evil thoughts, murder, adultery, sexual immorality, theft, false testimony, slander" (Matthew 15:19).

It's only when we properly identify the source of lust as our own selves that we can take responsibility and do something about it.

Which brings me to an important point I don't want you to miss: Though the source of lust is our own evil desires, the One who is offended is God. When we choose lust, we are actively rejecting God:

> For God did not call us to be impure, but to live a holy life. Therefore, he who rejects this instruction does not reject man but God, who gives you his Holy Spirit. (1 Thessalonians 4:7–8)

After David had committed adultery with Bathsheba, and even had her husband murdered, he recognized his sin as first and foremost against God. He cried out to God:

> Against you, you only, have I sinned and done what is evil in your sight, so that you are proved right when you speak and justified when you judge. (Psalm 51:4)

David's sin affected others—he violated Bathsheba and murdered her husband—but ultimately he saw that his sin was an expression of rebellion, even hatred, against God. This isn't true of just adultery; all sin is active treason against a holy God.

When we understand that the very nature of lust is rebellion against God, we realize the gravity and the serious nature of the sin—and hopefully we're more motivated than ever to pursue a life of purity.

WHEN ENOUGH IS NEVER ENOUGH

In the first chapter we read Ephesians 5:3, which says, "But among you there must not be even a hint of sexual immorality, or of any kind of impurity, or of greed."

But why is God's standard so high? How can God demand not even a hint of lust when He knows that He made us with strong sex drives?

One of the reasons God calls us to cleanse our lives of lust completely is because He knows that lust never stays at the level of "just a hint."

Lust is always an unholy desire for the forbidden. But though lust longs for an object or a person, ultimately this object is not its prize; its goal is the very *act* of desiring. The result is that lust can never be quenched. As soon as the object of lust is attained, lust wants something more.

In Ephesians 4:19, Paul describes this endless cycle of lust. He speaks about those who have turned away from God and says, "Having lost all sensitivity, they have given themselves over to sensuality so as to indulge in every kind of impurity, with a continual lust for more."

That's the payoff of lust—"a continual lust for more."

Even when you indulge in *every* kind of impurity, you're still filled with a continual lust. You won't be able to fantasize enough to quench lust. You won't be able to sleep with enough people. You won't be able to view enough pornography. You can gorge yourself on lust, but you're always going to be hungry. You'll be trapped in a never ending pursuit of wrong desires—always reaching for something that cannot be grasped.

God says *"not...even a hint"* because you can't give in to lust's demands and hope to pacify it. It always grows. And as it does, lust will rob you of your ability to enjoy true, godly pleasure. You can't bargain with lust and come out a winner.

EMBRACING YOUR SEXUALITY

As you read the coming chapters, keep this radical but liberating idea in mind: God *wants* you to embrace your sexuality. And battling lust is part of how you do that.

Does the idea of embracing sexuality and fighting lust sound contradictory? That's probably because today's culture offers a very narrow definition of what it means to embrace your sexuality. It equates embracing your sexuality with doing whatever feels good. So according to our culture, to deny a sexual impulse at any point is to be untrue to yourself.

But there's a big difference between embracing sexuality and *indulging* it. Indulgence doesn't lead to the satisfaction of lust any more than if you were to indulge a child's every whim. The spoiled child wouldn't wake up tomorrow and want less. As C. S. Lewis noted, "Starving men may think much about food but so do gluttons; the gorged, as well as the famished, like titillations."

As Christians, embracing our sexuality looks radically different. We don't obey every sexual impulse—nor do we deny that we have sexual desires. Instead, we choose both restraint and gratefulness. For us, sexual desire joins every other part of our lives—our appetite for food, our use of money, our friendships, our dreams, our careers, our possessions, our abilities, our families—in bowing before the One True God.

In other words, to rightly embrace our sexuality we must bring it under the dominion of the One who created it. When we do so, we're not fighting against our sexuality; we're fighting *for* it. We're rescuing our sexuality from being ruined by lust. We're exalting our God-given identity as sexual creatures by refusing to be trapped in the never ending dissatisfaction of lust.

When we embrace our sexuality and claim it for holiness, we are true to who God made us to be. He made us to be holy. In holiness we find the best and ultimately most deeply satisfying expression of our sexuality. And in holiness we experience the truth of what God made.

And what He made is *good*.

chapter three

You Can't Save Yourself

Where Can I Find the Power to Change?

I once read the true story of a duke named Raynald III, who lived during the fourteenth century. His sad life illustrates how giving in to our lustful desires—the very thing we often equate with freedom— actually robs us of freedom and true joy.

Raynald III had lived a life of indulgence and was extremely overweight. In fact, he was commonly called by his Latin nickname, Crassus, which means "fat."

After a violent quarrel, Raynald's younger brother, Edward, led a successful revolt against him. Edward captured Raynald but did not kill him. Instead he built a room around him in the Nieuwkerk Castle and promised him he could regain his freedom as soon as he was able to leave the room.

This wouldn't have been difficult for most people since the room had several windows and a door of near-normal size, and none was locked or barred. The problem was Raynald's size. To regain his freedom, he needed to lose weight. But Edward knew his older brother, and each day he sent him a variety of delicious foods. Instead of dieting his way to freedom, Raynald grew fatter. He stayed in the room for ten years, till his brother died in battle. But by then his health was so ruined that he died within a year— a prisoner of his own appetite.

Many men and women today are prisoners to their appetite for lust. Like Raynald, they look free, maybe even happy. They're doing what they want. They're doing what feels good. But the sad truth is that every bite of lust's delicacies only makes them more of a prisoner. When we indulge in a life of sin and do whatever feels good, we're not free. We've slaves to our sin.

IN JAIL WITH OUR APPETITE

In today's world we celebrate self-made people who can pull themselves up by their bootstraps. So when we hear that we're imprisoned by lust, our first thought is to orchestrate our own jailbreak. But like poor Raynald, we can't save ourselves.

In chapter 1 we examined the importance of having the right *source of power* to change and the right *motive* for fighting our sin. Only the power of the gospel can rescue us from the prison of our sin, and only the motive of grace can sustain us in the ongoing struggle against lust. Getting these two wrong will derail our efforts. When our motive is wrongly based on earning God's acceptance and our power is our own will, everything we do to overcome lust will backfire. Why? Because in essence we'll be trying to save ourselves.

We need to examine this tendency to try to save ourselves. Because if we don't address this faulty thinking now, everything I say to you in the coming chapters—all the practical strategies for fighting lust—will be worthless. They'll only take you further from where you need to be.

Here's what I mean. Out of a desire to overcome and conquer lust, you might be inspired to commit yourself to a rigid set of rules for accountability—for what you will and will not watch, read, or listen to. In and of themselves, these commitments might be very good. But what I learned from my experience with "the contract" is that rules and regulations that stem from self-righteous and self-centered motivations can actually take us away from God. John Owen taught that trying to put our sin and lust to death based on our own human strength is the "essence and substance of all false religion in the world." Even a good guideline for fighting lust, if it's "carried out with man-made schemes, always ends in self-righteousness."

Recently a nineteen-year-old college student named Jay told me about a system he and his friends had created to help fight the temptation to look at pornography. If one of them sinned in this way, all the others had to go without food to "take the punishment" for the sinning party. "It's been a little over four weeks now, and more brothers have joined us in our battle against lust," he wrote. "With more people's food intake based on whether or not I choose to sin, the decision to flee from it gets easier and easier day by day."

I love Jay's genuine desire to overcome his sin. And I can only commend him for taking lust seriously. But ultimately I don't think his system by itself will work any better than our contract did. Law can never bring about deep, long-lasting change. Jay and his friends need to be rooted in the life-transforming truth that someone has already "taken the punishment" for them. Jesus Christ bore God's wrath for every one of their sins when He hung in agony on the cross. This is the good news of the gospel.

Here's what you have to remember: You need to be rescued. You need God's grace. And not just on your bad days—you need God's grace *every day*. There's a name for this process of trying to save yourself like Jay is and like I did years ago. It's called legalism.

LEGALISM AND LUST

When my friends and I drafted our contract, we had some good motivations behind our guidelines. But we were pursuing holiness divorced from an understanding of what Jesus had accomplished for us.

This is the essence of legalism. Often we think of legalism as applying the wrong set of rules. But that's not necessarily true. Legalism is using any set of rules—bad rules, good rules, even God's laws—in a wrong way. In his book *The Cross Centered Life,* C. J. Mahaney writes, "Legalism is seeking to achieve forgiveness from God and acceptance by God through my obedience to God."

Legalism is trying to add to what Jesus did when He died and rose again. Legalism is seeking to relate to God based on our work, instead of based on the work of our representative and mediator, Jesus Christ.

Christ died to set us free from the tyranny of all our human contracts, which seek to make us righteous before Him. The law, and our obedience of it, could never make us righteous. It only reveals how sinful we are and how incapable of changing by ourselves. The law is a huge sign-post pointing out the fact that we need a Savior.

Please don't base your battle against lust on legalism. It never works. You'll either become hopelessly disillusioned at your failure, or if you succeed, you'll become puffed up with self-righteous pride. Your legalism might appear to produce results for a while, but ultimately it will work against your pursuit of holiness.

If you were to use the practical ideas I'm about to share with you as a legalistic set of guidelines, not only would it be displeasing to God, but you wouldn't change. Your behavior might change for a while, but your heart wouldn't change.

You'd crash and burn. It would all be drudgery. You'd start looking for ways to circumvent your own rules. Holiness would seem dry and boring and lifeless. And sin would become more enticing and even more powerful.

That isn't the life Christ died to give you. "It is for free-dom that Christ has set us free," Paul writes. "Stand firm, then, and do not let yourselves be burdened again by a yoke of slavery" (Galatians 5:1).

Two Important Words

An important part of standing firm in the gospel and avoiding legalism is understanding the difference between the work *Christ* accomplished to save us and the work of becoming holy that He enables *us* to participate in after we've been saved. Theologians assign the terms *justification* and *sanctification* to these two closely related but different concepts.

C. J. Mahaney gives the following definition of each:

- *Justification* refers to your status before God. When you placed your faith in Jesus, God the judge handed down the verdict that you are righteous. He transferred the perfect sinless record of Jesus to you. God completely and totally forgave you. He not only wiped away the record of your sin; He credited the righteousness of His Son to you.
- *Sanctification* is a process—the process of becoming more like Christ, of growing in holiness. This process began the instant you were converted and will not end until you meet Jesus face to face. Through the work of His spirit, through the power of His Word, and through fellowship with other believers, God peels away our desire for sin, renews our minds, and changes our lives. This ongoing work is what we call being sanctified.

Why do these theological terms even matter? Because they have everything to do with God's plan for changing sinners like you and me.

Too many people confuse the process of sanctification with God's declaration of justification. In other words, they think that their work at becoming holy and fighting lust is what saves them. No! The process of sanctification is the result of being justified. *Nothing we do in our pursuit of holiness adds to our justification.*

All the necessary and important aspects of pursuing holiness don't add to our salvation; they're the *response to* and the *result of* God's finished work of justifying us. Christ died so that we could be freed from the hopeless task of trying to justify ourselves. We no longer have to grovel in obedience under the rule of our human contracts, or what John Stott calls our "systems of merit."

Our obedience cannot earn our forgiveness. Our sorrow cannot pay for our sins. Our tears cannot cover them. No amount of self-inflicted punishment can make us right before God. Even our own death is not enough.

There is only one solution: to believe on Jesus Christ. To renounce all hope in our own ability to save ourselves and to place our faith in His ability to save us.

FORGIVEN IN FULL

Justification is a finished work. We don't have to hold our breath wondering what God thinks of us. When you turn from your sin in repentance and through faith in Jesus ask for forgiveness, God forgives you. Period. Don't let anyone tell you otherwise.

At times when I'm more aware of my sin than I am of God's grace, I'll quote the lines of a hymn we often sing at our church called "Before the Throne of God." The second verse strengthens my soul:

> *When Satan tempts me to despair,*
> *   and tells me of the guilt within,*
> *upward I look and see Him there*
> *   Who made an end to all my sin.*
> *Because the sinless Savior died,*
> *   my sinful soul is counted free;*
> *For God, the Just, is satisfied*
> *   to look on Him and pardon me.*

Yes, there is guilt within. But Jesus has made an end of all my sin! Don't let this truth get away from you. Focus on this reality. Don't doubt your forgiveness. When you feel condemned and separated from God, you're more likely to turn back to lust for comfort, and that's certainly not what

God wants you to do. Don't let anything distract you from the rock-solid reality that when God forgives, you're truly forgiven. When you sin for the millionth time and then in true repentance cry out for mercy, when you do what you promised you'd never do again and call out to Him with genuine faith in His grace, God forgives.

My friend Eric Simmons has taught me to insert my name into Psalm 32:2: "Blessed is Joshua Harris, whose sin the LORD does not count against him." Put your name in there. If you've trusted in Christ, it's true of you too. What an incredible truth! Because of Jesus' death for us, God does not count our sins against us.

Free to Be Holy

But does this mean we can cheat God? Since we're forgiven and justified, does that mean we can sin all we want? *Absolutely not.* If you've truly been justified, you're going to want to be sanctified too. You're going to want to begin growing in holiness. The person who has experienced God's grace and has been genuinely converted can still choose to sin, but he can't love sin like he used to. He can't continue in sin indefinitely.

Our freedom is not a freedom that leads to sin and selfishness, but to righteousness and love.

Galatians 5:13–14 says:

You, my brothers, were called to be free. But do
not use your freedom to indulge the sinful nature;
rather, serve one another in love. The entire law is
summed up in a single command: "Love your
neighbor as yourself."

Freedom from the law doesn't mean that we no longer
obey God. "On the contrary," writes John Stott, "although
we cannot gain acceptance by keeping the law, yet once we
have been accepted we shall keep the law out of love for
Him who has accepted us and has given us His Spirit to
enable us to keep it."

The gospel frees us to do what we were originally created to do: enjoy and glorify God with our whole lives. The
gospel sets us free to be holy.

LED BY THE SPIRIT

Both legalism and indulgence in sin imprison us. But when
we place our faith in Christ, God frees us from both and
gives us His Spirit to lead us into the freedom of holiness.

Have you ever heard people talk about being "led by
the Spirit" and wondered what this really means? The

Spirit-led life is not some superspiritual or mystical state; it simply means walking in step with the Spirit. It should be the experience of every Christian. It's the Holy Spirit who enables us to change, to resist sin, to apply God's Word to our lives. So the Spirit-led life is one submitted to the direction, agenda, values, and priorities of God's Spirit, as illuminated through Scripture. It's a life of freedom and holiness!

Without God's Spirit, our lives are marked by erratic compulsions—one day committing to a strict contract of rules, the next day bingeing on sin like Raynald in his self-made prison cell. Trying to live the Christian life guided by our fallen human nature is hopeless. It usually consists of the futile attempt to obey God in our own strength one moment and then giving up altogether and running after sin the next. But the result of walking by the Spirit is very different. Galatians 5:22–25 says:

> But when the Holy Spirit controls our lives, he will produce this kind of fruit in us: love, joy, peace, patience, kindness, goodness, faithfulness, gentleness, and self-control. Here there is no conflict with the law.
>
> Those who belong to Christ Jesus have nailed the passions and desires of their sinful nature to his cross and crucified them there. If we are living

now by the Holy Spirit, let us follow the Holy
Spirit's leading in every part of our lives. (NLT)

Do you see the better life God is calling us to? God isn't
just saving us *from* sin; He's saving us *for* a life of love, joy,
peace, patience, goodness, and self-control. Yes, there's sacrifice involved. The call to follow Jesus is a call to put our
sin to death, to crucify it and then let the Holy Spirit control *every* part of our lives—including our sexual desires.
He asks us to give up chasing the lustful desires that could
please us temporarily. Yet on the other side of that sacrifice
is freedom and true pleasure.

A SOLID PATH

We can't save ourselves and we can't change ourselves. Only
faith in Christ can rescue us from the prison of our sin. And
only the Spirit can transform us. Our job is to invite His
work, participate with it, and submit more and more of our
thoughts, actions, and desires to Him. We'll examine what
this participation should look like in the coming chapters.

Picture the Spirit-guided life as a proven but narrow
path winding between two deep ravines. The safe path of
grace and Christian freedom travels between the treacher-
ous pits of legalism on one side and indulgence in sin on

the other. For centuries, misguided people have twisted Scripture to justify leaving the path of freedom for one or the other.

In a similar way, this book you're holding could be misused. One person could apply its practical examples and advice for putting sin to death in a legalistic manner. Another person could take its emphasis on grace and forgiveness as an excuse to indulge in sin.

I hope you won't make either of these mistakes. Ask for the Holy Spirit's help. Reject the lie that you can add to what Jesus did in dying for you. Place your faith completely in Christ's substitution for you, and make your pursuit of holiness a response to His grace.

You've been called to freedom—the freedom of holiness. Jesus died to set captives free, not only from the law, but also from indulgence. The pure and wide-open air of freedom is just beyond the doorway. Are you ready for it?

Part Two

In the Thick of the Battle

chapter four

A Custom-Tailored Plan

Where Am I Weakest and What Can I Do?

One night my friend Andrew and I went to rent a video. At the door to the video store he stopped and said, "I'll wait out here."

"Why?" I asked.

"I don't want to go in," he said. He explained that God had convicted him about looking at the explicit covers of many videos. His way of fighting back was not even to enter.

I know Andrew felt a little silly standing outside the video store. I'm sure people must have thought we were strange as I brought different videos to the window to have him help me make a selection! But that didn't matter to Andrew. He was seeking to be obedient to what God was showing him about his own areas of temptation.

A lot of people can admit that lust is a prevalent sin in their life and say they want to change. But unlike Andrew, they've never taken the time to think through how the process of temptation unfolds for them. Instead of anticipating and being on their guard, they're surprised by the same attack over and over. I've been guilty of this myself.

Do you know precisely where your weak points are? And more important, do you have a specific plan not only for defending yourself, but also for actually taking proactive measures to protect yourself from lust?

I want to walk you through the process of identifying the specific ways *you* struggle with lust so you can create your own "custom-tailored plan" for overcoming lust.

YOUR PROBLEM IS UNIQUE

Each of us is unique in how we're tempted to lust. This shouldn't be a surprise—we all have different backgrounds, different weaknesses, and different sinful tendencies. All these combine to make us particularly vulnerable to lust in certain situations.

This is why there can be no "one size fits all" approach to combating lust. That's also the reason it would be a mistake to evaluate how you're doing in this area by comparing yourself to others. It's possible to think you're "above lust" just because you're not struggling with it like someone else you know.

But lust is manifested in each of our lives in a different way. Should you feel proud that you've never looked at Internet porn, while your eyes soak up sensual images on TV? Should you feel smug that you don't masturbate, while you keep going further and further in your physical relationship with your boyfriend? Is God impressed that you only watch PG-rated movies if your thought life is X-rated?

One man in his mid-thirties who heard me share this principle told me how God used it to open his eyes. "When certain friends expressed struggles with staring at women who were immodestly dressed, I thought, *Grow up! Don't be so weak,*" he said. But then he began to see just as much lust in his life. "While my lustful thoughts are not as common as some, they are just as bad and are made worse by my pride. My lustful desires are to gain attention from certain women at the office. I desire them to desire me."

Do you see how our sin can deceive us into feeling safe? Often those who feel the safest are the most at risk.

Paul warns us in 1 Corinthians 10:12, "So, if you think you are standing firm, be careful that you don't fall!"

This is why we can't deal in generalities or comparisons when it comes to resisting temptation. If we want to make progress, we have to be focused on our own unique weaknesses.

And then we must decide not to gratify them…

IDENTIFYING LUST TRIGGERS

After getting migraine headaches for the past several years, I discovered they were triggered by certain foods. The headaches didn't come immediately after I ate these foods, but over time things like caffeine, chocolate, and certain preservatives would build up in my system and then trigger a bad headache that would lay me out for days at a time. As I've learned to avoid those foods, my life has improved greatly.

There's a principle here for our fight against lust. Unfortunately, lust springs from our own sinful hearts—we can lust without any outside influences. But I've found that certain seemingly insignificant sinful compromises can build up in my system. My bigger outbreaks of sin are usually triggered by smaller sins that I wasn't diligent in guarding against. I'm talking about the daily, even hourly decisions of what to watch, read, listen to, and allow my mind to think about and my eyes to rest upon.

Romans 13:14 is a guiding verse for me: "But put on the Lord Jesus Christ, and make no provision for the flesh, to gratify its desires" (ESV).

When I think of "making provision," I picture my wife packing lunch for each member of our family on a day trip. Do you make provision for lust? In your small, daily choices, are you actually caring for and feeding your weaknesses and lust triggers?

In times when I'm tempted, I'll say to myself, "Don't pack a lunch for lust!" I must not pamper or provide even a little snack for the lust of my heart to feed on.

Richard Baxter wrote, "Keep as far as you can from those temptations that feed and strengthen the sins which you would overcome. Lay siege to your sins, and starve them out, by keeping away the food and fuel which is their maintenance and life."

Lust is kept alive and our weaknesses are fortified by the small provisions we give it. Think about it for a minute. Where are *you* weak? What are your lust triggers?

Here are a few categories to consider:

Time of day

Are you more susceptible to lust at certain moments in your day? Right when you wake up or go to bed? At the end of work, when you're tired and tempted to feel sorry for yourself? Weekends, when you lazily sleep in and are less disciplined? Many people I know find time in the bathroom a consistent temptation.

Think through how you could better prepare yourself for these moments. Many people have found that meditating on Scripture before they fall asleep helps set their mind on spiritual things and makes them less likely to indulge in sinful fantasy. Other people set up a phone call with a friend at the times they know they're weak. Others find that praying and listening to worship music in those weak moments help.

Tempting locations

Are there certain *places* where you're more tempted by lust? The mall? A bookstore where you're tempted to wander into the wrong sections? A friend's house where you know there's pornography? A part of your town where there's more chance of seeing immodestly dressed men or women?

Limit your time in these locations or stop going altogether. When you do have to go to these settings, go only with much prayer and even accountability from a friend who will ask afterward how you did.

After a vacation to a certain beach in Florida one year, I decided I couldn't go back. The water was great, the beach was beautiful. But it was also crowded with women in revealing swimsuits. Shannon and I talked about the temptations and the next year found a more isolated beach to visit. It wasn't as nice, but I wasn't sinning every day and had a much better time.

The place where you're weak might not be an area where other people you know are weak. That's okay. Don't worry about what others think or whether or not they understand. Just obey God.

Television

In chapter 7 we're going to look at the role media plays in our struggle against lust. For now I just want to ask whether you're an active or passive viewer of television.

My pastor C. J. Mahaney has taught me by example the importance of "active remote" television viewing. TV watching is not a spectator sport—with split-second accuracy, you have to be ready to change channels, zap commercials, or even shut the whole thing down.

This year I was with C. J. and a group of friends watching the Super Bowl. I don't think I saw more than two commercials the whole time. C. J. had the remote, and as soon as commercials came on he'd switch to C-SPAN, possibly the safest channel available. Why does he do it? Doesn't he know how entertaining and interesting the commercials during the Super Bowl can be? Yes, and he also knows how often they use sex to sell their products. He knows that nothing he might miss is worth exposing himself to lustful images.

In these moments it's easy to rationalize watching. I've had the thought, *Well, it's just a commercial. It's going to be over in a few seconds. It can't be that bad.* But that's a lie. A sinful image can lodge itself in my mind in much less than thirty seconds. At times when I've traveled and stayed at hotels I have sinned against God by mindlessly surfing through the channels. I don't necessarily stop and view something sinful, but I surf by it knowing there's a good chance something will flash before my eyes. God has helped me to see my own sinful desire in those moments. Even though I'm just flipping by, this is an expression of lust. Because of my poor track record, I've made it my habit not to even turn the TV on in a hotel.

My friend Joe refuses to watch TV by himself. If his wife Esther isn't there, he does something else. What steps do you need to take to honor God in the way you watch TV?

Newspapers and magazines
Are you careful about what you read? Today newspapers and magazines are spiced with content designed to stir up lust. Even if no photographs accompany the article, our lust can be fed by gossip about the love lives of celebrities, an article about sexuality that minimizes sin, or a short

story that paints fornication in an appealing light. It might not seem like a big deal, but it all adds up.

For some, obeying God in this area means not reading certain magazines at all. One guy I know realized that he couldn't pick up his mom's *People* magazines because of the immodest pictures. Another guy skips the "Style" section of the newspaper because it frequently features articles and topics that tempt him. A girl named Natalie averts her eyes from the covers of tabloids and women's magazines when she's buying her groceries. "Those magazines tell me I need to look like sexy celebrities. I don't want to buy those lies so I look straight ahead at the cashier. I count coupons! I find a way to keep my mind from being filled with images and ideas that directly attack biblical femininity and purity."

Music

Good music can move our hearts to love God; ungodly music can entice us to love sin. No person is immune to the influence of music with sinful content. The musicians we listen to become our companions, and God says the companion of fools will suffer harm (Proverbs 13:20).

Who are your companions? What's in your CD or MP3 player? Is it helping or hindering your fight against lust? So much of today's music—regardless of the style—celebrates and encourages lust. And I'm not even talking about the way the artists dress or present themselves in their videos—the lyrics alone can encourage wrong desires. Don't let a good beat or a catchy melody justify listening to music that presents sin as good. Reprogram your radio settings in your car. Throw out some CDs. Listen to music that draws your heart to God.

Books

Many women I know have been convicted of making provision for lust by reading romance novels. "It started for me when I was twelve," a nineteen-year-old girl named Kelsea wrote me. "I wasn't experiencing romance in my own life and desperately wanted to, so I turned to what I call 'soft porn' romance novels."

The effect of this reading diet wasn't good. "I was having really perverse thoughts," she confessed. The scenes of illicit passion she'd filled her mind with were leading to impure desires.

Kelsea repented and threw away her books. After that she began to read Christian romance novels, but even then she found herself tempted. "The sex scenes aren't at all graphic in a Christian romance, but just the whole romance thing would bring back other scenes I'd read in secular novels. Lately I've come to the realization that I can't read any of it," Kelsea said. "It's been hard, but I've noticed that by not reading any romances—and fasting and praying—the lust in my mind is really coming under control. Praise God! I still have lapses, but they are much fewer than before."

Internet

For many men and women, the Internet isn't just a little battle; it's the main battleground where they're tempted daily to indulge in lust. Escaping this temptation requires radical action. If this is your situation, don't lose hope. Please keep reading. Many men and women have found victory over this specific temptation.

If you're not struggling with on-line pornography, that's good—but please don't assume you're safe. If you're not willing to fight the little battles of purity today in this area, you'll more than likely end up ensnared in something bigger in days to come.

"I used to go on-line to look at pictures of what fashions the celebrities were sporting at the latest awards show," a girl told me. "It wasn't porn and wasn't originally sought for the purpose of feeding lust, but I realized that the combination of all the skin I was seeing and the lifestyles represented was not helping me love God." So she stopped.

Are you flirting with lust on-line? Are there websites you visit that feature images or content that, though not pornographic, excite sinful desire in your heart? Stop going there.

Don't allow sin to gain a foothold. Be radical. Don't go on-line alone late at night or at any time when you're feeling weak. One guy I know cancelled his Internet access altogether. I know other people who always have their computer facing toward the door so others can see what they're viewing when they walk by. Some use software that automatically e-mails a list of all the sites they visit to an accountability partner.

The mailbox

I don't know about your house, but at our home all kinds of sensuous and provocative clothing catalogs arrive in the mail uninvited. I've come to realize that I have to view even getting my mail as a battleground. Will I throw them away immediately, or steal glances and flip through them for a quick thrill?

I've fought back in several ways. First, I've asked my wife, Shannon, to help keep these kinds of catalogs out of our home. She often gets the mail and sorts it. She has even called certain companies and asked them take our address off their list. If you're a guy with a similar struggle, ask your wife or mother to help you in this area by ridding your home of these unnecessary temptations.

Girls need to be careful too. "My roommates and I

throw out the questionable catalogs right away," Grace told me. "Not only do we not want that stuff laying around when our guy friends come over, but we want to protect ourselves from the body envy that results from poring over them. That's not God's definition of true beauty and we shouldn't allow it to become ours."

In public

My friend Bob describes summer as a time for "staring at the sidewalk." Sometimes when you're out in public, the sidewalk seems like the only place you can look without being tempted to lust after someone. But regardless of the season, immodestly dressed men and women are always going to be around us. We have to choose to honor God with our eyes and not gaze on others lustfully.

A girl named Tatiana told me how God showed her that her "harmless" pastime of checking out guys was really a dangerous hobby, fueled by lust. Another girl named Lauren confessed, "I have never been in a relationship in which my eyes haven't wandered, looking for something better. It truly scares me, because I know if I don't stop now I'll do it even after God blesses me with a godly husband. This is a real struggle for me. I literally have to look the other way."

Because this is such a daily temptation, it might seem easier to just give up or relax your standards. Don't do it.

You *can* obey God with your eyes. You can avert your gaze. You don't have to take a second look or let your eyes linger on someone.

It helps me to remember that my eyes are actively obeying my heart. They don't have minds of their own. They're obeying me. So it's my job to command them to obey God. They don't have to see everything around them. If an attractive girl walks by, they don't have to survey her body. But they must obey Jesus Christ. I've offered my eyes to God to be used in His service. Because Jesus died for me, my eyes are no longer tools in the service of sin—they can and they must obey God (see Romans 6:13).

ACT ON WHAT YOU KNOW

Have you recognized any lust triggers in your own life? This list of course isn't exhaustive. Even if your specific struggle isn't listed, you can still work to identify where you battle lust.

Take a few minutes to formulate your own custom-tailored plan for fighting lust. Grab a piece of paper or your journal:

1. List your own top three lust triggers. How can you avoid them?

2. What time of day or week are you most tempted by lust? What can you do to prepare for those times?

3. Which locations are the most tempting for you? How can you limit your time in those places?

4. What five little battles do you need to be fighting more faithfully? Describe in detail what it looks like for you to fight—and win—these battles.

Writing down your own custom-tailored plan can sometimes be discouraging. Sin looks worse when it's recorded on paper! But think about how much better prepared you'll be after this simple exercise. You'll be more aware of where you're weak and better prepared to resist lust. It's not a foolproof plan and doesn't remove your need to actively depend on God's Spirit. It's merely a way to cooperate with God's work in you.

You'll need to constantly update this information. The way you struggle with lust will change. There may be seasons when something you were never tempted by before becomes a serious issue. Be ready for that possibility and respond quickly.

And remember that it's not enough to merely feel bad about or dislike the consequences of lust. True repentance is a change of direction. It involves turning away from sin and toward God—replacing sinful actions with righteous ones. Genuine repentance springs from heartfelt sorrow over sin because it is against God and then leads to real change in the way a person thinks and lives. My friend and fellow pastor John Loftness has created a helpful list of seven steps called "The Path of Repentance" that walk through this process. I've included the list in this book as an appendix.

You must be willing to take specific and dramatic action. Are there things in your home you need to throw away? Are there habits you need to end decisively today? Be radical for the sake of holiness. Jesus said, "And if your right hand causes you to sin, cut it off and throw it away. It is better for you to lose one part of your body than for your whole body to go into hell" (Matthew 5:30). Jesus used an extreme example to illustrate how we must be willing to do whatever it takes to avoid sin.

I faced this kind of difficult decision with my membership at a local gym. I had signed up for a yearlong commitment and started working out in the mornings. But a few weeks later I knew something had to change. I was consistently being tempted, and was often succumbing to the temptation to look lustfully at women.

For me this was an important battleground. I prayed about it and felt strongly that God wanted me to take radical action and stop going. I'll be honest. This was a difficult decision for several reasons. First, because I still had to pay for a full year of my membership at the gym. But also because many of my Christian friends were members and they weren't struggling to guard their eyes like I was. It wounded my pride to admit that I couldn't handle being there. I wanted to be above the temptation. But I wasn't. So I stopped going and started working out at home.

Is there something God wants you to cut out of your life? Act on what God is showing you. Don't be deceived and think that reading this chapter has changed anything about your life—change will occur as you obey. It's not enough to hear truth and agree with it; we have to do what it says (see James 1:21–22).

START WITH ONE THING

But what if there are a hundred things you need to act on? Once, after speaking to a group of college students about fighting the little battles against lust, a young woman approached me with a sincere question. "I want to do what you're talking about," she said, "but it seems like I'll have to think about this stuff all the time. Won't I go crazy?"

The little battles can seem to be everywhere, and you might feel overwhelmed. Where does a person start?

The truth is that we can't deal with everything at once. That's why my advice is to pick one area to begin working on. Choose a specific item from your list to make your focus. Take it to God in prayer. Repent of your apathy toward sin and determine what obedience would look like.

Then seek to be faithful in that area. Take it seriously. Pray about it. Fight the little battles. Flee temptation. As God gives you grace to change in that area, you can move on to another area.

What you don't want to do is feel so overwhelmed by all the lust in your life that you're paralyzed. Just take one step at a time. Your steps might seem insignificant, but they're not. God is rejoicing over even the smallest act of obedience. And as you humble yourself and cry out in prayer for His assistance, He will give you more and more grace to change. Keep your eyes fixed on Jesus. "Consider him who endured such opposition from sinful men, so that you will not grow weary and lose heart" (Hebrews 12:3).

Don't grow weary. Consistency in the little areas will slowly strengthen you spiritually. Just as compromise adds up, so your faithful investments into holiness will grow too.

chapter five

Guys and Girls

*How Are We Different,
and How Can We Help Each Other?*

When I gave the message that originally inspired this book, I was addressing an all-male audience. But my first words were humorously directed to any woman who might try to listen to a tape recording of my talk. "Let's get something straight," I said with a grin, "this message is *not* for you!" The audience of men howled.

"And don't give me the excuse that you want to 'understand your brothers,'" I continued. "No, you just turn it off."

The guys could relate to how embarrassing it would be to have women listening in on our "men only" session on lust. We were sure that if girls really knew how we struggled with impurity they'd write us off as a bunch of sex-obsessed animals. Among men it's a common understanding that lust is a guy thing and girls just can't relate.

But within days I received requests from many women who wanted to listen to it on tape. Several planned to discuss it in small group settings. They heard guys talking about the message and wanted to listen themselves—and not because they wanted to "understand" men but because they too struggled with lust.

I suppose this shouldn't be that surprising—sin is sin, after all. But I thought men had a monopoly on lust. I've learned that men and women have more in common than you might think. In this chapter, I want to examine what men and women have in common when it comes to lust, how we're different, and how we can help each other.

Let's begin by debunking the most persistent misconceptions we have about each gender.

Women Struggle Too

When it comes to lust, the greatest misconception about women is that they only deal with lust on an emotional level. Over the years many Christian books (my own included) have emphasized that men struggle with physical desire and guarding their eyes, while women deal with their emotions. But if these generalizations aren't qualified, people might get the impression that women *never* struggle with lust as raw physical desire, or that their struggle against lust is less real. This just isn't accurate. "Women have sex drives too!" a woman named Katie wrote me. "Believe me, as a twenty-two-year-old virgin, I know."

My goal isn't to convince anyone that women lust just as much as or in the same way as men—ultimately it doesn't really matter. But many women struggle with lust in what you might call traditionally male ways—the temptation to view pornography, to masturbate, to focus on the intense physical desire for sex. These women are often hindered in their fight against lust because they're consumed with shame over the particular ways they struggle. "It feels like a guy thing to be battling," one girl said.

"There is an amazing lack of resources for women on this subject," Cara wrote me. "We don't have seminars on it. There's a haze around the issue of female lust, and women need to understand the roots of their struggle."

Another woman named Kathryn said lust seemed like a taboo subject among her Christian girlfriends. "Sometimes I get the distinct impression that I'm the only Christian female with this problem," she explained.

You're not the only woman to face physical lust. God's Word says, "The temptations that come into your life are no different from what others experience. And God is faithful. He will keep the temptation from becoming so strong that you can't stand up against it" (1 Corinthians 10:13, NLT).

Women, it doesn't matter if your sex drive is as strong as a guy's or how it compares to other girls you know. What matters is whether or not you're looking to God for strength to control the desires you have. What matters is whether or not you're fleeing temptation and pursuing holiness because you love Him.

ARE ALL MEN MONSTERS?

A major misconception about men is that their problem with lust is much worse and more serious than any woman's could be. In other words, that men are monsters while women are innocent and pure.

The truth is that men's lust is more obvious, but not necessarily more sinful. Guys are typically more visually oriented, and as a result their lust is more visible. And because God made men to initiate and pursue women, their expressions of lust are often more aggressive and blatant.

But here's the question: Is a guy's lust, which is blatant and obvious, worse than a girl's lust, which is more refined and subtle? A nineteen-year-old girl named Stacey doesn't think so. She wrote me the following letter about how God has convicted her of many of the "harmless" female expressions of lust.

In the past year or so, I have realized just how much my mind is trained to lust over guys' looks. Guys can be just as much objects of lust as women. If I could count how many movies my friends and I have gone to see simply because there was some cute celebrity in it, I'd be ashamed at the number. And then there are TV shows and magazine covers. Our whole culture thinks it's perfectly normal for girls to drool over hot guys—in fact, it encourages it. I spent three years in high school being a fanatic of a certain boy band member who will remain nameless. I went to countless concerts, screaming and running up, trying anything to get closer to the stage. If that's not lusting, I don't know what is. I was reducing a guy's worth down to only how physically attractive he was.

It's not helpful to think that a girl who lusts as she watches a romantic comedy is less disobedient than a guy who thrills over an R-rated movie that contains nudity. Both are indulging in lust.

My point is that none of us should feel safe because our expressions of lust are culturally acceptable or civilized. I'm not saying this to excuse any man's sin or let anyone off the hook. The point is not that guys aren't so bad. The point is that *all lust is bad*. Apart from God's grace working in us and changing us, we're all monsters. Regardless of how lust is expressed, it's motivated by a sinful desire for the forbidden. Lust is always based on the same lie—that satisfaction will be found apart from God.

How Are We Different?

Though we have a lot in common, God has made men and women gloriously different. We were made to complement each other. We have different strengths. We are "wired" differently sexually.

When it comes to the differences between men and women, the following statements are generally accurate and may be helpful to consider:

- A man's sexual desire is often more physical, while a woman's desire is more often rooted in emotional longings.

- A man is generally wired to be the sexual initiator and is stimulated visually; a woman is generally wired to be the sexual responder and is stimulated by touch.
- A man is created to pursue and finds even the pursuit stimulating; a woman is made to want to be pursued and finds even being pursued stimulating.

Isn't it wonderful how God has made men and women to interact with each other? He made men visually oriented, then made women beautiful. He made men initiators, and then designed women to enjoy being pursued. In the heart of each man is an innate desire to romance and win the affection of a woman. God plants a longing in a girl's heart from a young age to make herself attractive. All this is part of God's wonderful design.

Understanding God's plan helps us see where lustful desires will seek to sabotage the original purpose. Lust always starts with something good—like a mirror at a carnival, it takes God's design then distorts it.

PLEASURE AND POWER

Lust blurs and bends true masculinity and femininity in harmful ways. It makes a man's good desire to pursue all about "capturing" and "using," and a woman's good desire to be beautiful all about "seduction" and "manipulation." In general it seems that men and women are tempted by lust in two unique ways: men are tempted by the *pleasure* lust offers, while women are tempted by the *power* lust promises.

At the heart of a guy's temptation to lust is often a desire for sensual and physical pleasure. The payoff of lust for a guy is that it will feel good. A man's lust leads him to detach a woman's body from her soul, mind, and person and use her for the sake of his selfish pleasure. Isn't this why most pornography is directed toward men and depicts women presenting themselves solely for a man's pleasure? Pornography reinforces the lie that women are sexual playthings for men's enjoyment—that women want to be used, not loved and cherished. Some men prefer to masturbate to pornography over engaging in a real relationship with a woman because it allows them to live in the fantasy that their own physical pleasure is all that matters.

Of course, a woman can be tempted by lust in a similar way. But lust doesn't seem to come quite as naturally to a woman. What does come naturally is a desire for intimacy. So when a woman sees a seductive ad featuring a man, she might be tempted to fantasize about sex with him, but the odds are that this temptation will be rooted in fantasy about a *relationship* with him, with physical pleasure being a subset of her craving for passionate attention and emotional intimacy.

Lust offers men the pleasure of sex devoid of the hard work of intimacy. Lust offers women the power to get what they want relationally if they use their sexuality to seduce. Dr. Al Mohler once made a shocking yet accurate statement: "Men are tempted to give themselves to pornography—women are tempted to *commit* pornography." If you're a woman, you don't have to pose for a picture or star in a pornographic movie to commit pornography. When you dress and behave in a way that is designed primarily to arouse sexual desire in men, you're committing pornography with your life.

"I believe that the root of women's struggle with lust is that we want to dominate men, control them, and manipulate them through sexual appeal," a married woman from Knoxville wrote me. "If a couple is driving down the street and they both see a very seductive advertisement, they can both be tempted toward lust but in different ways. The man might be tempted toward sexual pleasure with the woman in the ad. But women want to look like the woman in the ad because we know men want that."

A woman named Josie agrees. "There is a degree of power in seduction, even though it is short-lived and false. Women know we have the ability to make a man do what we want by dressing or acting in a certain way."

Diane avoids lingerie ads and storefront displays. Because of her past sexual sin and because she used to dress seductively in order to attract guys, seeing those images triggers anger and frustration. She has realized that one way a woman acts out lust is to incite lust in men.

How are you tempted? Recognize that these temptations are often interchangeable between the genders. We can all be tempted by the pleasure and power lust offers. But understanding how men and women often gravitate toward one or the other can help us create our own custom-tailored plan for fighting back. Once we identify the specific lie our lustful desire is telling us, we can counter this false promise with specific truth from God's Word. In chapter 9 we'll look at the promises of Scripture. For now it's enough to understand that we must meet these specific temptations with the truth that God alone can give us lasting pleasure and that only He can satisfy our desire for intimacy.

HOW CAN WE HELP EACH OTHER?

Because we're most often the source of temptation for each other, I believe men and women can do a lot to encourage each other in our common pursuit of holiness.

I do *not* mean that men and women should keep each

other accountable about lust. In fact, I would strongly discourage a man and woman from talking about lust together unless they're engaged or married. Our hearts are deceptive, and talking about this with a person of the opposite sex can often invite temptation. So men should be accountable to men, and women to women.

All that being said, we can do so much to help one another. Our interaction with the opposite sex can strengthen their resolve to flee temptation. Second Timothy 2:22 says, "Flee the evil desires of youth, and pursue righteousness, faith, love and peace, along with those who call on the Lord out of a pure heart." Paul told Timothy to pursue godliness with other Christians. This is to be our goal as Christian men and women.

For guys

Let's start with how guys can serve their sisters. We need to take into account the three statements listed above about female sexuality:

- Their desire is often rooted in emotional longings.
- They're stimulated by touch.
- They're excited by being pursued.

These facts need to shape the way we interact with women. We have to take these characteristics seriously.

Have you ever interacted with an immodestly dressed girl and really wished she had a clue about how much her clothing affected you? Well, as a guy you need to realize that certain things you do and say to girls are the equivalent of male cleavage—they just aren't helpful to our sisters. We need to get a clue!

Probably one of the most important things godly single men can do to help their single sisters is to actively be brothers to them. Don't flee relationships with them. Helping to guard their purity doesn't mean avoiding them. It means caring for them and extending genuine friendship. We can encourage Christian women we know who are serving God passionately. We can thank women who dress modestly.

And finally, we can pray for our sisters. Do you ever pray that God would help the women you know to find their satisfaction in Him? Take the time to pray that God would help them love holiness and avoid the wrong visions of femininity the world constantly offers them. Pray that God would help them be virtuous, not seductive. Your prayers and friendship will accomplish more than you can imagine.

For girls

You can help guys in their fight against lust by being aware of just how *aware* guys are of your body. Rarely a moment goes by when a guy isn't aware of your body. And you don't have to have a cover model's body for this to be true. If you're a woman, this applies to you. This should affect how you clothe yourself as well as how you interact physically with guys. One girl I knew in high school was completely oblivious to how much her friendly, full-on frontal hugs affected guys. Girls, don't hug guys like this! My friend Nick, who secretly liked this girl for two years, called them "breast hugs" and anticipated receiving one each Wednesday at youth group. The girl was being friendly, but Nick was lustfully enjoying the opportunity to be pressed against her body.

When I say that guys are always aware of your body, I'm not implying that they're always lusting after any woman they're with (although this is possible). I mean that in any interaction with a woman, a healthy man is aware that you're a woman and that you have a body his sinful desires would love to lust after. A Christian man seeking to resist lust never reaches a state where he's unaware of a female's body. He just learns to actively choose not to stare. So a godly Christian guy really does (or really should) want to view you as a sister and maintain eye contact—not "eye to something else" contact. But when you wear clothing that accentuates, draws attention to, or highlights the feminine parts of your body, it's like wearing a flashing neon sign pointing to the very thing he's trying not to be consumed with. Sure, guys can resist the temptation to lust, and it's our responsibility to do so, but your dressing immodestly makes this very difficult.

I know that talking about flashing neon signs might make this sound like a joke. But immodesty really isn't funny. Ask God to help you see how selfish and uncaring it is to want to use your body to encourage your brothers to lust. It might make you feel good about yourself, but it could encourage them to sin. The way you dress can either help or hinder the men around you who are trying to resist lust.

My wife, Shannon, puts it well when she says that there's a difference between dressing attractively and dressing to attract.

Advice for couples

What if you're in a relationship? How does a couple help each other? First, recognize that lust is the greatest enemy of a healthy, godly relationship. If you love God and each other, determine to hate lust. Don't feed lust in your relationship. It won't stop wanting till your relationship is ruined. Maybe you've been in a relationship that was overrun by lust. If so, you know how the story unfolds. Lust keeps pushing. And every step along the way becomes less and less satisfying. Yes, there's immediate pleasure. But it's a pleasure that leaves you with a deep gnawing desire that won't go away.

Sadly, what many couples discover is that lust doesn't stop prodding them after they've "gone all the way." There is no such thing as "all the way" with lust. Ultimately, lust doesn't want sex. It wants the forbidden, and it's willing to take you deeper and deeper into perversion if you'll indulge its latest request.

If you're dating or even engaged, please don't bargain with lust, assuming it will go away after you're married. If you feed lust now, it will only grow. It will want more. Don't compromise before marriage—whether you're a week or year away from the wedding. God wants you to guard the marriage bed (Hebrews 13:4). Sexual release is not the antidote to lust. If you think it is, you've got a sad surprise coming—lust will be waiting for you after your honeymoon with a whole new batch of lies.

Is your relationship gripped by lust? Step back and take a break from the relationship. Does God want you with this person? If after prayer and counsel from godly men and women, you both feel God wants you together, commit yourselves to purity in a radical way. If possible, make a beeline for marriage, cut out the physical completely, and involve other godly couples in your life. You *can* choose to honor God with your bodies. Just because you've been involved physically in the past or even slept together doesn't mean holiness no longer matters.

My first two books include chapters that address this in great detail. You can read them by yourself or as a couple. If you can't afford to buy them, just go to a bookstore and read the chapters titled "The Direction of Purity" in *I Kissed Dating Goodbye* and "True Love Doesn't Just Wait" as well as "When Your Past Comes Knocking" in *Boy Meets Girl.* I hope you find them helpful.

In This Together

Lust seeks to use what we know about the weaknesses of the opposite sex to manipulate them. Isn't it wonderful that as brothers and sisters in Christ we can use this same information to help each other pursue holiness?

Our membership in God's family must transform our view of the opposite sex. We're not trying to get something from each other: we're called to give, to love, and to care for one another. The opposite sex shouldn't be viewed as a bunch of potential partners—they are men and women created in God's image, whom Christ died to save. They're family! We are given not only the responsibility but also the amazing privilege of looking out for each other—even fighting and sacrificing for each other. This is what true love is all about. First John 3:16 says, "This is how we know what love is: Jesus Christ laid down his life for us. And we ought to lay down our lives for our brothers."

Can you imagine the righteousness that could be born if we're willing to lay down our lives for each other? Can you picture the glory we'll bring God as we stop seducing and using each other and begin guarding and protecting? Because Christ freed us from the power of sin, we don't have to give ourselves to pornography or commit pornography—we can give ourselves to holiness and commit acts of purity as expressions of worship to God and love for others.

chapter six

Self-Centered Sex

How Do I Deal with Masturbation?

In case you're looking, this is the chapter about masturbation. Don't feel bad if you were looking for it. I've done the same thing. I've picked up a book on sexual purity, browsed the table of contents, and immediately turned to the chapter titled something like "The *M* Word" or "What About Masturbation?"

Why go there first? I guess because I want to know the author's opinion. I want someone to help me figure this out. It isn't exactly a topic you casually bring up. A lot of men and women I know can barely bring themselves to say the word. "Can I just call it 'self-stimulation'?" one guy asked me in an e-mail.

Regardless of what we call it, masturbation is something the vast majority of men and women deal with on some level. In fact, many find themselves trapped in a cycle of defeat and shame. They try to stop, but they can't. They promise God they'll never do it again, but they fail. Masturbation becomes the defining issue in their relationship with God. They're desperate for answers—are they doing something wrong, or should they just give up trying to resist?

Because Scripture doesn't specifically name the act of masturbation, a heated debate has erupted among Christians, and there is an endless array of opinions on the issue. One Christian book will say it's wrong, another that it's perfectly fine. One expert will say it's healthy, another that it's destructive. There are even dozens of pro-masturbation and anti-masturbation Christian websites making their cases on the Internet.

Can we draw any clear conclusions? Can we know the truth? I believe we can. Because even though you won't find the word *masturbation* in the Bible, God's Word does address this issue and gives us everything we need to deal with it. Scripture clearly speaks of the danger of lust and shows us what it means to have an accurate view of sex.

BIG DEAL OR NO BIG DEAL?

Is masturbation a trivial issue that we need to stop worrying about so much? Or is it a big deal?

I think it's both. Let me explain. First, I think Christians make too big a deal of masturbation in that we obsess over the act and neglect the more important issues of the heart. No question, God is concerned with our actions, but He's even more interested in our motivations. Men and women I talk to are often consumed with how many times they've masturbated, but I think God wants us to be more concerned with the soil of our hearts, out of which a lifestyle of masturbation grows.

It's a mistake to make the act of masturbation the measure of our relationship with God. I remember a stretch of nearly a year when I was in high school during which I didn't masturbate. I felt pretty good about myself. But in hindsight, my smugness was ridiculous. I may have stopped masturbating but during the same period I was indulging my lust in a sinful physical relationship with my girlfriend. We made out multiple times a week. I was dishonoring her and disobeying God's commands for purity. And yet I ignored this clear compromise, thinking that God was impressed that I wasn't masturbating.

If you believe that masturbation is wrong, do you minimize other sins as a result? For example, when you detect arrogance or see self-righteousness in your life, do you respond the same way as when you mess up? Do you live under a cloud of shame and feel you can't approach God till you've paid penance? Most of us don't feel this way. For some reason we're usually able to acknowledge these other sins, repent, and believe that Christ's sacrifice was enough to pay for them. We know we might sin again, but we choose to press on in obedience and trust God to help us.

So does this mean we should masturbate and not worry about it? No, that's not what I'm suggesting at all. I don't agree with those who say that since it's difficult for most not to masturbate and since God surely doesn't want us to feel guilty all the time, masturbating must be okay. We could apply this same bad logic to numerous other habits that are hard to resist. God's solution for our guilt is not to change His definition of sin. God dealt with our guilt at the cross of Christ: "For Christ died for sins once for all, the righteous for the unrighteous, to bring you to God" (1 Peter 3:18). Even when we sin again and again, we can find grace again and again. And the power of God's Spirit can help us to grow in obedience.

So when I say we shouldn't make too big a deal of masturbation, I mean we shouldn't make it the primary barometer of our spiritual lives. Lust is a serious sin. Masturbation is one expression of a lustful heart. But when we inflate the importance of this act, we'll either overlook the many evidences of God's work in us or we'll ignore other more serious expressions of lust that God wants us to address.

WHY IT MATTERS

The reason this very private act matters to God is not because it involves our genitals, but because it involves our hearts. And God is passionately committed to our hearts belonging completely to Him (see Deuteronomy 6:5).

Masturbation isn't a filthy habit that makes people dirty. It only reveals the dirt that's already in our hearts. It's an indicator that we're feeding the wrong desires. That's why problems with lustful actions are symptoms of deeper heart problems.

Now you might be thinking, *What are you talking about my heart for? This is about my sex drive and is purely biological. Don't even little kids do this before they're old enough to lust?*

Hear me out. I'm not ignoring the biological realities involved with this issue. It's true that God has made us sexual creatures with bodies that have the capacity and the urge to satisfy themselves through self-stimulation. Many of us figured out this trick before we were old enough to know what it was called. And as we grow into adolescence, these natural drives only increase. There's a real, physiological component to all this that shouldn't be ignored. A guy's body produces semen that at some point has to be released. This is why a male who doesn't masturbate will have wet dreams where semen is released during sleep. The majority of males are most sexually charged before sex in marriage is even an option.

So in a sense, masturbation is natural. But does natural mean good? As Christians we have to be careful about assuming that something that comes naturally to humans is morally insignificant. We live in a fallen world. Every part of this planet and our humanity has been marred by sin. So though none of the natural functions of our bodies are inherently sinful, we have to be aware that natural desires can easily become sinful cravings.

Because of sin, even if masturbation starts out inno-cently in a child, it inevitably begins to involve lustful desires and fantasy. For most people the act is impossible to separate from lust in the heart—whether this involves pornography or not. One guy told me that he and his friends use the acronym LIA to refer to masturbation. It stands for "lust in action."

I know there are Christians who claim they can mastur-bate without lusting. They say they think nonsexual thoughts and do it merely for release. It's not my place to judge the hearts of these people. I can only speak from my own experience when I say that I highly doubt this is pos-sible. What I've seen is that lust was always present in a significant way either leading up to or during the act. And then I think of Jeremiah 17:9, which says, "The heart is deceitful above all things and beyond cure. Who can understand it?" In light of my own ability to lie to myself, I'm very hesitant to trust my own evaluation, especially on this topic. Maybe I can convince myself I'm not lusting in that moment, but the likelihood is that my heart is deceiving me.

New Thinking

Even if it were possible to masturbate without lust, I think a lifestyle of masturbation is based on a wrong understanding of God's plan for sex.

Masturbation is built on a self-centered view of sex. This wrong attitude says that sex is solely about you and your pleasure. Your body. Your genitals. Your orgasm. This is the natural tendency of sin. It isolates us from others and makes pleasure self-focused. When our lustful desires are given free rein, sex is pushed into a corner and made a completely self-centered, isolated experience that reinforces a self-centered view of life.

If you want to break free from a pattern of masturbation, the first step is to renew your understanding of sex. You must embrace a God-centered and selfless attitude toward sex.

What does this mean? First, it means acknowledging that sex belongs to God. He created our sexuality and is the only One with the authority to dictate how it should be expressed. Sex is for Him. All that we do as sexual creatures should be an expression of our honor, love, and fear of Him.

Second, a God-centered view of sex strives to honor God's purpose for sex. It's not enough to know God's *rules* for sex. We need to understand His *purpose* and *plan* for it.

WHY DID HE CREATE IT? WHAT WAS HIS INTENT?

Marriage and sex are inseparable in God's design. You can't have one without the other. In Hebrews 13:4, when God addresses our attitude toward sex, He starts by adjusting our view of marriage:

> Marriage should be honored by all, and the marriage bed kept pure, for God will judge the adulterer and all the sexually immoral.

This passage tells us that a healthy attitude toward sex starts with a high view of marriage: "Marriage should be honored by all." To honor something means to hold it in high esteem or to respect it. God is telling us that before we can view sex accurately, we have to take marriage seriously. We have to understand that in God's sight, when a man and woman marry and join their bodies together sexually, something spiritual occurs—they really do become "one."

When a husband and wife make love, it is a living picture of the spiritual reality of marriage—two people melded into one. But this physical joining is only one part of the union. Marriage is the combining of a man and woman at every level—not just sexually but emotionally, spiritually, and in every other way.

In God's plan, sexual union was never meant to be separated from this total union. C. S. Lewis compares having sex outside of marriage to a person who enjoys the sensation of chewing and tasting food, but doesn't want to swallow the food and digest it. This is a perversion of God's intent. Food was meant to be chewed and also swallowed. In a similar way, the sex act was meant to be a part of the whole-life union of marriage. When we attempt to experience sex apart from this union, we're disrespecting and dishonoring marriage.

Jeffrey Black writes, "The goal of pornography and masturbation is to create a substitute for intimacy. Masturbation is sex with yourself. If I'm having sex with myself, I don't have to invest myself in another person. People who are 'addicted' to pornography aren't so much addicted to lurid material as they're addicted to self-centeredness. They're committed to serving themselves, to doing whatever they can to find a convenient way not to die to self, which is the nature of companionship in a relationship."

If you cultivate a habit of masturbation, don't assume it will end once you're married. I know many married people who continue to be tempted. Sometimes "solo sex" seems easier, even more pleasurable, than the work involved with maintaining intimacy with your spouse and unselfishly seeking to give him or her pleasure. But a husband or wife who turns to masturbation in marriage becomes a rival to his or her own spouse. The act of masturbation draws them away from each other.

That's why my wife, Shannon, and I have committed to each other not to substitute masturbation for sexual intimacy even if we're away from each other. We want sexual pleasure to be something we're dependent on each other to experience. We want sexual desire to be something that draws us together as a couple.

WHY NO MEANS YES

When God says no to something, it's because He's saying yes to something better. In His infinite mercy, God wants what is best for us. Let's just look at the facts:

- God wants us to live in joy and freedom. But masturbation leads to spiritual enslavement—when we give in to the urge to masturbate whenever we want, we're setting ourselves up to become slaves to our desires. And giving in to masturbation makes it harder to say no to other forms of lust. The cycle of defeat and enslavement sets us up to expect and cave in to sin in other areas of our life. Second Peter 2:19 says, "For a man is a slave to whatever has mastered him."

- God wants us to learn to control our bodies in holiness and honor (see 1 Thessalonians 4:3–6). But masturbation is like a dragon that grows stronger over time and requires more and more food. And it likes variety. Once you commit to feeding it all it needs to feel the ultimate thrill, you'll find yourself having to indulge in more and more lustful thoughts and you'll end up looking for thrills in places you never expected to go.

- God wants husbands and wives to delight in sexual intimacy within marriage without shame. But masturbation done with guilty feelings and regret before marriage can color the way a spouse views sex itself. Having been on the treadmill of shame because of masturbation, a wife may find that later in marriage, sexual fulfillment feels tinged with shame. She's come to associate it with sin.

There are benefits to practicing self-control. God isn't keeping anything good from us. He's not just saying no. He's actually saying yes to the good.

Practical Help

Overcoming lustful masturbation begins with renewed thinking about sex. But you can also take some practical steps to change your habits. Here are a few ideas:

- Identify the specific times of day and locations in which you're tempted to masturbate. Prepare yourself for those moments and places in advance by praying and asking for God's help.
- Memorize key Scriptures. First Thessalonians 4:3–6 and Romans 6:12–14 are great (I've listed more in chapter 9).
- Meditate on Scripture as you fall asleep.
- Sleep with your bedroom door open.
- Get out of bed in the morning as soon as your alarm

goes off. Lying in bed and allowing your mind to wander is a recipe for failure.

- In moments of temptation, redirect your attention and do something else. Get out of your room, go for a walk, or call a friend.
- Be disciplined about your time in the bathroom and any reading material you keep there.
- Review the lust triggers you identified in chapter 4. If possible, get even more specific about what leads to masturbation and avoid those sources—TV, movies, or magazines—that inflame your desire.
- Don't play the "I'll touch myself but won't climax" game. Flee temptation by not touching yourself at all.
- Share your struggle with someone else. Sharing your struggle with a parent or trusted Christian friend is one of the best ways to overcome masturbation. Chapter 8 is all about the importance of accountability.
- Fill your time with activities that put your focus on serving and caring for others.
- Focus on the gospel. Consistently read Scripture and books that remind you of Christ's sacrifice for your sins. You cannot successfully battle any sin apart from an awareness of God's grace.

- Don't make masturbation the sole focus of your spiritual life. Ask God to show you other ways He wants you to grow besides this issue. Does He want you to grow in humility, in servanthood, in gentleness, in giving? Study and pray about these areas.

God is after your heart. That's what He cares about. He wants your undivided passion. As your mind is renewed by His Word and as you put away wrong thinking, lust's power will steadily weaken in your life. Set realistic expectations. Complete change will take time and effort.

Remember that God isn't impressed by vows (see Ecclesiastes 5:1–7). He wants you to humbly depend on Him and draw your strength from Him. What if you fail? Take God at His word and believe that the sacrifice of His Son is enough to forgive the sin of lustful masturbation. The Cross is more than enough to cover all your sin. And remember who receives your prayers. "For we do not have a high priest who is unable to sympathize with our weaknesses, but we have one who has been tempted in every way, just as we are—yet was without sin" (Hebrews 4:15). The one who understands your weakness is the one who perfectly obeyed God's law and who died in your place for your sins. Christ's perfect record has been transferred to us; His spotless righteousness clothes us (see 2 Corinthians 5:21).

START PLANNING

Let me leave you with a final piece of advice that you might find surprising. This may be misunderstood. It may even shock a few people. But I'll take the risk.

Here's my advice: Get married.

Unless God has removed your desire for sex and has given you a clear vision to serve Him as a single person, then assume that you're supposed to get married and either make yourself ready or begin pursuing it.

I know what you're thinking. *Is this coming from the guy who kissed dating goodbye?!* Absolutely. Directionless dating can be one of the biggest detours from marriage. Don't waste your time…go for it!

Now let me make a few qualifications. First, I'm not saying that your driving motivation for marriage should be that you want to stop masturbating. Second, I'm not addressing this to the fifteen-year-olds who are reading— you have to be mature enough for marriage to take this advice. Third, I'm not encouraging anyone to make a hasty or rash decision—I've written two books about the importance of wisdom and patience. Finally, I understand that there are many people who want to marry but haven't been able to. I'm sorry if you find this counsel frustrating.

With my qualifications out of the way, let me say that I think there are far too many singles today (men in particular) who have no good reason for delaying marriage.

Sometimes I think it's just plain laziness and selfishness. Other times it's a cultural, unbiblical emphasis on career and material success.

The world has abandoned marriage and commitment for a lifestyle of empty "hookups." Don't follow the world's pattern. Pursue God's gift of marriage. God has given marriage to us for our good. The world is increasingly delaying and avoiding marriage—we should do the opposite. No one should be ashamed to want to marry young and enjoy the wife (or husband) of their youth. Marriage is great. Sex in marriage is terrific! We're not just called to guard the marriage bed; I think more Christian singles should be running toward it!

Paul gave similar advice to unmarried people dealing with sexual desire: "But if they cannot control themselves," he said, "they should marry, for it is better to marry than to burn with passion" (1 Corinthians 7:9). God has given us marriage not merely as a concession, but a provision for our sexual desires. While it's true that sexual intimacy won't eliminate lust, God has given it to us to protect us from the temptation to indulge in fornication and sin. If you're burning with passion, God is calling you to marriage. Get yourself ready! Get your eyes (and hands) off of yourself, and pursue the sacrifice, love, responsibility, selflessness, and God-glorifying sex of marriage.

chapter seven

Half a Poison Pill
Won't Kill You

How Do I Cope with the Temptations of Media?

I *hope I don't see anyone from church.* I was walking up to the counter of my local video store when the thought flashed through my mind. My wife's mom was visiting us that weekend, and the ladies had sent me out in search of a movie. I didn't have any idea what to get. So there I was wandering the aisles of cleavage-covered video covers trying to find a "good" video in the midst of a lot of bad ones. There were several safe bets, a few classics

I could've chosen, but none seemed that exciting. I wanted something new.

That's when I happened upon the movie. My policy with movies is to get a recommendation from another Christian and check out the content of a film on-line before watching it. I didn't know anything about this particular movie, which should have been enough to make me pass it by. But that night I was more concerned with being entertained than sticking to my standards. I could bend my policy a little. Okay, so the wording of the description made it obvious there was sexual innuendo. *I'm an adult. I can handle that.* Surely it couldn't be that bad. Besides, I needed to get something and I couldn't spend the whole night searching.

I grabbed a copy and started walking to the counter. That's when the *hope-I-don't-see-anyone-from-church* thought came. That should've been an obvious signal that something was very wrong with my choice. My conscience had been whispering to me as I read the video case—now it was shouting at me. Deep down I knew the movie probably wasn't good. I knew I was compromising for the sake of entertainment. As I pictured bumping into a member of my church, I realized I wouldn't be able to recommend the video to them or even explain why I'd chosen it. God was convicting me, but I ignored it.

I handed my movie to the girl behind the counter. She

swiped my video card and stared blankly at the computer with my account information. Then her eyes lit up. I saw her silently mouth my name.

I cringed.

She looked up and said, "I know you! Are you the Joshua Harris who wrote that book *I Kissed Dating Goodbye?*"

I wanted to die.

ONE BIG "LITTLE BATTLE"

I'm sad to say that I rented the movie that night and watched it with my wife and mother-in-law. It was awful. The jokes were crude, it was packed with sexual innuendo and adultery, and we had to fast-forward through several scenes. I was even more embarrassed that the girl at the video store had recognized me. I'd never seen her in my life. And I never saw her working again. I honestly think God had her there that week just to remind me that even if nobody from church sees what I rent, He's watching. And I want to live in that reality every day.

When it comes to our entertainment choices, a lot of Christians are like I was that night at the video store—we're more concerned with what others might think than with what God thinks.

Growing up, I learned that Christians have a wide range of standards when it comes to TV and movies. Unfortunately, I used this fact as an excuse not to establish my own convictions before God. Instead of responding to His Word, I evaluated my media habits based on how they compared to other people's. Anyone whose standards were a half-step *lower* than mine was sinning, and anyone with standards a half-step *higher* than mine was probably legalistic and too uptight.

Of course, my standards were perfectly fine, and nobody needed to tell me otherwise. Can you relate? We don't like having anyone else tell us what we can and can't watch. If anyone tries, we put our fists up, ready to defend our viewing habits.

I hope you won't read this chapter defensively. I'm not going to tell you what you can and can't watch. I don't have an "approved" list of movies you can watch. But I do want to look at how we can practice biblical discernment and wisdom when it comes to our viewing habits.

This is an essential part of rooting out lust in our lives. Chapter 4 looked at how important the little battles are. And there's probably not a more important little battle than the daily decisions we make in the area of movies and television.

This is a very personal topic for me. In the past two years, God has begun to show me just how much my unhealthy media diet has fed my lust and negatively affected my spiritual life. What I've come to see is that no matter how much I study the Bible, pray, and ask God to help me conquer lust, I'll never move forward in holiness if I'm filling my mind with lustful images and ungodly themes through entertainment.

Straight for the Heart

Why does media play such a crucial role in our struggle against lust? Is it because of all the sex and nudity in today's entertainment? Well, yes, but there's much more at stake.

Today's media, especially television, seeks to define reality for us. It wants to tell us how to think about sex, about marriage, about our desires, about sin. The danger of not bringing God's standards to bear in what you watch isn't only that you might see a naked body, but that the values of a sinful world will shape what you're living for.

Entertainment goes straight for our hearts. Have you ever thought about this? Media never reasons with us in its attempts to convince us to love lust and sin. You'll never see the CEO of a television network standing in front of a flip chart explaining why adultery is good. But that same CEO might have his company create a television drama that engages your emotions and, through the power of the story, makes the sinful act of adultery seem appealing.

Television and film stir up feelings and emotions that bypass our minds and go straight for our affections. The incredible power of media is that it can make something evil look good or exciting without appearing to make any argument at all!

POISON PILLS

Here's the mistake I have often made. I know that media contains a certain amount of sinful content that is dangerous. But instead of seeing how much I can *avoid,* I spend my energy trying to see how much I can *handle.* I'm like a person who figures out he can take half a poison pill every day without killing himself. It's good that he's not dying, but can it be healthy to take all those halves of poison pills?

That's what I was doing that night in the video store. Instead of saying, "God, I want to honor You. I don't want to put something before my eyes that celebrates sin," I was saying with my actions, "Sin isn't that big a deal. I can take it in small doses."

What I'm starting to learn is just how important it is to evaluate the *overall* effect of my media diet. Too often I've been guilty of seeing the bad things I watch as a bunch of isolated incidents that aren't that detrimental to my spiritual health. But they're not isolated. They're all connected.

All those half-doses of poison are adding up and swimming in my blood. We need to examine the cumulative effect of our media habits on our attitude toward God, toward sin, and toward the world.

We should avoid graphic sex scenes in movies and television. But we also need to make sure the constant barrage of seemingly harmless entertainment isn't trivializing sin. So just because someone doesn't watch R-rated movies doesn't necessarily mean he's "safe." Today's popular sitcoms, and many PG-13-rated movies (and even PG-rated movies), can be extremely detrimental to our souls over the long run. Even if they don't contain graphic nudity, they can slowly and subtly undermine biblical truth and conviction in our hearts.

WHAT IS SIN?

So what are we allowed to view? It's easy to latch on to a rating system or some set of rules that will make it clear what we will and won't watch. But no rating system based on content can replace a heart that wants to please God. If we're to honor God with our entertainment choices, we must be willing to carefully evaluate how what we watch affects our love for God. We must be willing to wrestle with our standards and often refuse to watch what others think is permissible.

When he was in college, the famous evangelist John Wesley wrote a letter to his mother asking her to give him a clear description of sin. I think he wanted a list of do's and don'ts. But Mrs. Wesley didn't give John what he wanted. She gave him something much better. In response, she wrote:

> Take this rule: whatever weakens your reason, impairs the tenderness of your conscience, obscures your sense of God, or takes off the relish of spiritual things; in short, whatever increases the strength and authority of your body over your mind, that thing is sin to you, however innocent it may be in itself.

It doesn't matter what something is rated, or how popular it is, or how seemingly innocent it appears. If it hardens your heart toward God, if it obscures your awareness of the ugliness of sin and the holiness of God, if it takes the edge off your spiritual hunger, then it's sin.

CAN YOU THANK GOD FOR IT?

The issue is not that we avoid any portrayal of sin—the Bible is full of stories about the sinfulness of humanity. But, as writer Joel Belz points out, there is a right and wrong way for sin to be portrayed.

First, he writes, "A portrayal of sin should never prompt the reader or viewer only to want more of the same. Today many images of sin that should produce repulsion instead produce attraction." There's a big difference between reading in Scripture about David's adulterous affair with Bathsheba, which is condemned and shown to be wicked, and watching an adulterous affair in a film that is celebrated and made to appear good.

The next test is the one I find the most challenging. "If God's Spirit is not to be grieved," Joel Belz writes, "you should be able to honestly give thanks to God for the portrayal in its totality. This is not a simplistic test, but wholesomely biblical. If you can't bow your head and sincerely thank God for a movie or a symphony or a newscast or a novel—then for you that activity is wrong. Stop arguing with yourself, and move on to something else."

MORE THAN DISAPPROVAL

We need to grow in discernment. But we have to realize that discernment is more than just disapproval. Imagine if a friend who was on a diet said it was okay for him to eat chocolate cake since he didn't really like it. "If you don't enjoy a calorie, it won't make you fat," he reasons.

How would you respond to this logic? You'd probably laugh at his wishful thinking. It doesn't matter if you don't like a certain type of calorie—if that calorie is going in your body, it's going to have an effect!

And yet this is how we often practice discernment when it comes to our entertainment choices. We seem to think that because we don't approve, because we sigh and roll our eyes, because we complain about the ungodliness of Hollywood, because we fast-forward through the *really* bad parts, we can watch all the garbage in the world and our souls won't be affected. We call this "discernment." But that's as foolish as saying that if you don't enjoy a calorie, it won't make you fat.

True discernment is very different. First Thessalonians 5:21–22 says, "Test everything. Hold on to the good. Avoid every kind of evil." If our discernment doesn't lead to appropriate action—either holding on to or avoiding— it's worthless. Biblical discernment involves bringing God's standards to bear in our evaluation of what we watch and responding accordingly—whether this means refusing to watch something, refuting its message, or agreeing with it.

Are you testing? Are you avoiding every kind of evil? Are you holding on to the good? Remember, media is after your heart. It's not trying to reason with you—it seeks to disguise its message so that you'll welcome it and let your guard down.

WHAT SHOULD WE AVOID?

In his excellent book *Worldly Amusements,* Wayne Wilson describes worldly entertainment as that which does at least one of the following:

1. *Promotes an evil message.* It presents evil as good. This can be done by celebrating sins, such as lying, stealing, murder, fornication, or adultery. Sin is presented in an attractive way.
2. *Uses an evil method.* Regardless of the point of the story, the performers are made to behave in ways that are shameless and immoral. A story may lead to the conclusion that adultery is bad, but if we must wallow through a sea of flesh to reach this conclusion, the work qualifies as worldly.

No matter how excellent the production or acting, no matter how true the moral of the story, if something promotes an evil message or uses an evil method, the discerning Christian will avoid it. And it doesn't matter how many awards it has won!

So often we act as though knowing all about the sinful

content of the latest TV shows and movies is sophisticated or part of being relevant in our culture. That's not what God says. God says, "not...even a hint." In Ephesians 5:11, He tells us to "have nothing to do with the fruitless deeds of darkness, but rather expose them." But we can't expose the darkness of the world if we're lost in it ourselves. We have to be light. We can't speak to our culture or help rescue others from the darkness if we've allowed it to shape our thinking and values.

In Psalm 101:2–4, David says to God:

> I will be careful to lead a blameless life—
> > when will you come to me?
> I will walk in my house with blameless heart.
> > I will set before my eyes no vile thing.
> The deeds of faithless men I hate;
> > they will not cling to me.
> Men of perverse heart shall be far from me;
> > I will have nothing to do with evil.

That's the banner I want hung over my TV or any movie screen: "I will set before my eyes no vile thing." Why? Because I want to know God. I don't want anything to draw my heart away from Him. I want to love holiness.

Jesus Christ died to rescue me from darkness and sin. How can I willingly immerse myself in that darkness for the sake of entertainment? What a tragedy it is that I've sat idly by during movies and television shows and watched the very sin for which Christ had to die being laughed about, even celebrated.

Even if I could somehow prove from Scripture that I'm allowed to watch this, why would I want to? Why would I want to gain enjoyment or soak my mind in the sins that Jesus had to shed His blood to free us from?

CHANGING OUR HABITS

I know that many of these ideas are hard to swallow. It was through preparing a message for my church that God first began to convict me. I was supposed to be the preacher, preparing to challenge the congregation, but as I read God's Word and studied, it was like God put His hand on my shoulder and said, "Josh, you're the one who needs to change."

For me the process of overhauling my entertainment habits was sweet yet agonizing. I could see that God Himself was working in my life. He was pruning dead branches from me and helping me learn to better honor and obey Him. But it wasn't easy. To be honest, I liked a lot of those old branches. My thoughts easily reverted to wanting to figure out how much poison I could get away with ingesting. More than a few times I'd have thoughts like, *Oh no! Does this mean I won't be able to see the sequel to my favorite movie?*

But as I humbled myself and kept digging in to God's Word, I knew that changing my media diet was essential. I'd gotten into habits of renting movies so often that I was often bending my own standards because I "needed" to find something to watch. So I've started to wait until there's a film worth viewing—something for which I can thank God—before I go to the movies or rent something. The result is that I'm watching a lot fewer movies. Now when I do, it's more of a treat and I've found I'm more discerning about what I view. I've also found that lust has far less strength.

I've also cut out most television. My wife and I had gotten into the habit of watching a weekly show that often featured the main female character in immodest outfits and ungodly situations. It was having a deadening effect on my soul. It was also drawing us into other shows that were advertised and creating an appetite for more. We cut off our little routine and put the TV in the basement. Now we read a book together or visit friends. Life's been so much better.

I've seriously cut back on all of my media intake. And you know what? I've been okay. Sometimes we treat entertainment as if it's some kind of right, something essential to our existence. But it isn't. There is no such thing as "must-see TV." And if we're the only people in the world who don't see the latest summer blockbuster movie, we'll be all right. The only thing that's essential is walking with God and pleasing Him. And if that sometimes requires cutting back on what we watch, it's no real sacrifice.

Part Three

STRATEGIES FOR LONG-TERM CHANGE

chapter eight

Lone Rangers Are Dead Rangers

Why Is Accountability So Important?

I'm the last person you'd expect to fall into sexual impurity," twenty-three-year-old Trina says. Back home she was always the strong one. She led a Bible study for women in her church and was respected for the stand she took on purity. Her own life was living proof that purity was possible.

But then the job opportunity in Seattle came. It was

too good to pass up. At least that's what Trina thought at the time. She loved her church and hated the thought of leaving the close relationships and the solid teaching she enjoyed there. But she was sure it wouldn't be too hard to find a replacement in Seattle. She was wrong.

She visited a dozen churches, but none had the kind of biblical teaching she had grown up with. A year later she was attending a large Bible study for singles on Tuesdays and alternating between two congregations on Sundays—and sometimes she slept in and didn't bother going at all.

It just wasn't the same. She felt disconnected and lonely. At home she had enjoyed close relationships with three older women who knew her inside and out. They could tell when she was struggling just by looking in her eyes. Now they were fifteen hundred miles away.

Unlike many of her friends, Trina wasn't seduced by lust through a relationship, but through what started as a seemingly godly desire for marriage. "As I thought more and more about marriage," she said, "I began thinking of the wedding night, and because I was alone, that course of thought just continued to draw me in more and more. Instead of realizing that I was making marriage and sex a false god in my life, I gave myself up to lust."

For Trina, the wake-up call came when she sought out pornographic websites on the Internet. "No one who knows me would ever believe I would do that," she says. "I can't believe the mess I got myself into."

Easy Targets

Alone, isolated, and without accountability, Trina was the perfect target for temptation. Our enemy goes after people who have isolated themselves from other Christians. Stragglers make easy victims. Without other people to encourage them, watch out for them, and confront small compromise in their lives, they often end up drifting into serious sin.

Trina never realized how much of her spiritual strength was a direct result of the support and care she received from her local church. She took the weekly teaching, the relationships, and the accountability for granted.

What will it take for you to achieve lasting success in battling lust? There's nothing more important than being connected and accountable in a local church. If you want to experience long-term victory over lust, you must lock arms with other believers.

No matter how strong you might feel right now or how much victory over lust you're presently experiencing, you won't make it very long on your own. In the battle against lust, lone rangers wind up dead rangers. They might look impressive riding off into the sunset by themselves, but when an ambush comes they're without help (see Ecclesiastes 4:9–10, 12).

WE NEED EACH OTHER

The Christian life is something we do *together*. In Ephesians 4:29, God tells us to build each other up with our words, and later He instructs us to "speak to one another with psalms, hymns and spiritual songs" (5:19).

We need other Christians to speak, sing, and sometimes shout the truths of God's Word to us. We need others to pray for us when we're in the midst of temptation. We need friends who will hold on to us when we're ready to give up. We need friends who will challenge and even rebuke us when we're indulging in sin.

Are you connected to others in a local church? Many people today—especially young adults—have lost their vision for the church. I used to be one of these people. I thought of church as merely a building or a place to go for social interaction. I always went to church, but my lifestyle revealed what a low priority it was for me. The church was something on the outskirts of my life.

But God's Word says, "The church...is not peripheral

to the world; the world is peripheral to the church. The church is Christ's body, in which he speaks and acts, by which he fills everything with his presence" (Ephesians 1:23, *The Message*). The church is at the center of God's plan; it definitely shouldn't be on the outskirts of our lives.

Many people I know aren't willing to commit to a local church. They hop from church to church. Or they'd rather just find a Bible study or campus ministry. Though these settings can be good, God wants us to be connected to a local church and under the spiritual leadership of pastors and elders. Without this we won't grow.

If you're not part of a church, make it your top priority—even if you're away at school. Don't merely sample from a number of churches in your area; find one to which you can be committed. Ask God to help you find a strong Bible-teaching (and Bible-living) church where you can build relationships, serve, and be challenged to grow. (If you need help evaluating a church, my friend Mark Dever has written a book called *Nine Marks of a Healthy Church* that provides helpful biblical criteria.)

If you're in a good church, don't just attend—immerse yourself in the life of the church. If there's a process for becoming a member, dive into it. If the church has small groups, join one. Introduce yourself to the pastors. Let them know who you are, and communicate your support.

Volunteer to serve. Most important, seek to build real relationships with others. Don't wait for others to approach you. Be the one to take the first step.

Make Yourself Accountable

Once you're connected in a church, you need to make yourself accountable. We all need one or more close friends who we can involve in our personal battle against lust.

What does accountability look like? Alan Medinger gives this helpful description of what an accountability relationship involves:

> An accountability relationship is one in which a Christian gives permission to another believer to look into his life for purposes of questioning, challenging, admonishing, advising, encouraging and otherwise providing input in ways that will help the individual live according to the Christian principles that they both hold.

If you're in need of close accountability relationships, start by asking God to provide a godly man or woman with the same desire. What kind of person should you look for?

First, look for someone who fears God and who takes his word seriously. Don't settle for the person you feel most comfortable with; find someone who will make you uncomfortable in your sin.

If possible, it's best to be accountable to someone who is strong in the areas you're weak. Obviously this doesn't mean you have to find someone who never deals with lust. But neither should you look for someone who is currently sinning in all the same ways you do. Accountability works best when the other person is able to gently challenge you, not just relate to your struggle.

For teenagers it's ideal that accountability start with your parents. "I recently confessed to my dad about my ongoing fight with masturbation," a sixteen-year-old named Billy wrote me. "It was pretty humiliating, but I knew it was something God had laid on my heart. It unmasked pride in my life. And in the end it wasn't as embarrassing as I had imagined. My dad understood and has been praying and encouraging me ever since."

If your dad or mom is a Christian, talk to him or her about your temptations. God has given your parents to you to protect you and provide spiritual care for you.

It's also important that your accountability partner *not* be a member of the opposite sex. Even if you're just friends with a guy or girl, it isn't wise to discuss issues of sexual temptation with them. It often leads to temptation and inappropriate intimacy. One of the safeguards I established while writing this book was not to counsel or correspond with women about the topic of lust. I hired a Christian woman in my church to conduct all the interviews with women.

Finally, it's helpful for your accountability to have a structure and to be consistent. I meet with a group of four men every other Thursday for lunch. We each take time specifically to confess sin. It helps me to know that I'll be meeting with my friends every two weeks. Knowing that they'll ask me how I'm doing often helps restrain me in moments I'm tempted to sin. Even though I'm a pastor, I need accountability just as much as anyone else.

Once every two weeks might not be enough for you. Some people meet with their friend or small group every week. Others need a daily phone call for encouragement and support. Accountability can be flexible. The common goal is to help you and your partner or group do what pleases God and avoid sexual sin.

Women Need Accountability Too

Though accountability for sexual temptation is becoming more common among men, it's not as common among women. There are still many women who have never talked to another woman about this issue. But women need accountability on this subject too.

Please don't think you're the only woman dealing with lust. Don't let pride keep you from reaching out for help. You need other Christian women to come alongside you. Please don't hide your struggle or think that others will look down on you if you confess your sin.

I have male friends who face a similar temptation to withdraw from fellowship because they struggle with homosexual sin. They're terrified of what other guys will think of them. They're afraid that others will view them differently. So they keep it to themselves. But this only plays into the hands of the enemy. Cut off from fellowship and accountability, they only become more vulnerable to temptation.

Although it won't be easy, share your specific temptations with another woman. This can be any godly Christian woman you trust. If you're single, consider finding an older, married woman in your church in whom you can confide as well.

I think you'll be surprised at what an incredible release the simple act of confession brings. There's something about stepping out of isolation that begins the process of freeing a person from the chains of sexual sin.

First Peter 5:5 says, "All of you, clothe yourselves with humility toward one another, because, 'God opposes the proud but gives grace to the humble.'" Are you willing to clothe yourself with humility and share your struggles with another woman? When you humble yourself and take the step of confessing lust, God will give you more grace to battle that very sin.

Common Mistakes

Over the years I've learned from trial and error what makes an accountability relationship effective. Here are a few common mistakes to avoid:

General confession

Don't fall into the "vague confession" rut in your account-ability. General, broad categories of confession aren't help-ful. When it comes to lust, I've found that it's important to be very specific. If I withhold details from the men I'm accountable to, I limit the intensity of my own conviction and I limit my friends' ability to help me.

Allison was accountable with Christy and had con-fessed several times that she dealt with "impure thoughts." But it was difficult for Christy to know how to pray for Allison or counsel her on this issue. One day she asked Allison to be more specific. What were these impure thoughts? Where did they take place? Were they directed toward a particular person?

Allison humbled herself and told Christy that there was a man at her office she'd been flirting with for several months. He was making advances and she had been entertaining thoughts of immorality with him. Armed with this specific information, Christy was able to actually help Allison confront her sin. She held Allison to her promise to cut off the relationship. She knew how to pray for her. And in future conversations, Christy was able to ask Allison how she was doing in her thoughts toward the man.

My friend Ron, a thirty-six-year-old single man, has battled homosexual temptation since he was a teenager. God has helped him resist the temptation to act out these sinful desires, but for over twenty years Ron hid his struggle. "Because of my own fear of what other guys would think, I simply talked to them about generic lust and avoided specifically naming my sin. I continued this pattern of nonspecific confession for years." But then during a particularly low point in Ron's Christian life, God gave him the courage to break decades of silence. Ron confessed his temptation to a man in his church. It was like a great burden lifted off his shoulders. In the following week he shared with a pastor and another accountability partner. Now these men are able to better care for and encourage him. Specific confession has led to specific encouragement, specific accountability, and specific prayer.

Confusing confession with repentance

One common mistake I've often made is to assume that confession to my accountability group is the same thing as repentance. In other words, I would think that merely telling someone else I sinned meant I'd turned away from the sin and adequately dealt with it. But this isn't necessarily true. Repentance involves a change of heart and a decision to turn away from a sin. It's proven over time and involves an ongoing choice to put sin to death.

When you share your sin with others or listen to others confess sin, it's important to talk about what repentance looks like. Here are some helpful questions to ask:

- Do I view this sin as an act of rebellion against God?
- Is there true sorrow over my sin or do I merely dislike the consequences?
- Am I cultivating a hatred for this sin?
- What further action do I need to take?
- What will I do the next time I'm tempted in this way?
- What preemptive actions can I take to avoid this sin next time?
- What activities or thought patterns do I need to turn from?

Confession can be a helpful part of repentance, but it can't take its place. It's possible to feel bad about something and even tell someone else but not genuinely turn from our sin. Accountability relationships give us a chance to have others encourage us to demonstrate genuine repentance.

Offering sympathy but no challenge

Another common error in accountability relationships is what I call the "support group" mindset: When someone confesses sin, people offer sympathy but don't challenge the person. But we don't need to be consoled or comforted for our sin; we need to kill it!

I'm grateful to have Christian men in my life who love me enough to firmly challenge my sin. They urge me to put my sin to death. They remind me that God is holy and is opposed to my sin and that sin leads to death. They ask if I'm meditating on Scripture and crying out to God for help. They don't let me excuse or justify my sin.

Don't misunderstand, my accountability group is not self-righteous. They don't condemn me. They're very careful to encourage me. They always remind me that God is at work in my life. But they refuse to just affirm me and sympathize with me over my sin. They want to help me change and grow in godliness.

Confession with no follow-up

Confession doesn't equal change. That's why it's important in any accountability group or relationship that you follow up with each other. Tell your accountability group what to ask you the next time you meet. Ask them to revisit the area of temptation you've confessed. Ask them to be specific.

Here are the kind of specific follow-up questions I'm talking about:

- How did you do guarding your eyes at work today?
- Did you masturbate this week?
- Did you view pornography on-line this week?
- What are you meditating on when you wake up in the morning?
- Have you been memorizing Scripture to combat the lies of lust?
- Is your relationship with your boyfriend or girlfriend pure?

At times, follow-up might even take the form of a phone call. The important thing to remember is that accountability doesn't end with confession. We need to pray for each other and keep checking in with each other.

Gospel amnesia

The most important thing we can do for each other when we talk about sin and temptation is to remind each other of God's provision for our sin—the Cross of Jesus Christ.

Often, when a person is confessing sin, they're more aware of their sinfulness than they are of God's grace and mercy. It's a mistake to think that emphasizing guilt will lead to change. The opposite is true. It's only when we remember that God has forgiven our sin because of Jesus Christ that we can find the resolve to keep battling sin.

This doesn't mean we don't firmly challenge each other to forsake sin. It means we challenge each other in light of the glorious fact that Jesus has died for the very sins we're dealing with. In Romans 12:1, Paul wrote, "Therefore, I urge you, brothers, in view of God's mercy, to offer your bodies as living sacrifices, holy and pleasing to God." He urged them, but he urged them "in view of God's mercy" at the cross.

I encourage you to end each time of accountability with prayer marked by thanksgiving for Christ's work on your behalf.

SPURRING EACH OTHER ON

I hope this chapter has inspired you to make the local church a priority and to pursue accountability with others. "And let us consider," the author of Hebrews writes, "how we may spur one another on toward love and good deeds. Let us not give up meeting together, as some are in the habit of doing, but let us encourage one another—and all the more as you see the Day approaching" (Hebrews 10:24–25).

Some people give up meeting with Christians. They allow bitterness or the business of life to separate them from other Christians in a local church. It's a grave mistake. God's Word commands us to keep meeting together in the context of the local church. The Christian life is a race, but it's a race we run together.

chapter nine

The Power of
a Promise

How Can the Truth Help Me Defeat the Lies?

One day when I returned
home from work, my wife was gone and a stack of mail
was on the kitchen counter. I flipped through the bills.
Then I spotted a very explicit lingerie catalog at the bottom
of the stack. My pulse quickened. I snatched up the catalog and quickly twisted it into a tube, opened our back
door, and threw it into the trash can.

As soon as I shut the door, a very intense inner struggle

began. God had given me the strength to throw it away. But my sinful desire was lobbying hard. I'll be honest. I really wanted to open up that trash can and pull out the catalog.

A dozen thoughts and justifications flew at me: *Shannon is gone, so no one would know. I'll only look quickly. Maybe I could pick out some article of clothing for Shannon. That's it! I wouldn't be lusting; I'd be shopping! It's not pornography. I'll only do it this once.*

"No!" I said aloud. "I will not lift the lid of that trash can. I will not look at that catalog!" If my neighbors had seen me arguing with myself as I paced in our kitchen, they would have thought I was crazy.

But my lustful desires kept whispering: *It would feel good. You haven't done it for a long time. God will forgive you and you can find a humble way to confess it to your accountability group.*

The fact that I'd even think such deceitful thoughts scared me. I grabbed the phone and started calling friends. I dialed Joe…busy signal. Eric…answering machine.

Well, you've done your best to get help. You might as well indulge.

"Shut up!"

I dialed John's number and he answered. "Hey, Josh, what's going on?"

"Hey, buddy," I said with a sigh. "I need you to pray for me…"

WORN DOWN

It was God's mercy that I left the catalog in the trash that day. John's prayer and encouragement helped me weather the intense moment of temptation. But afterward something wasn't quite right. Instead of feeling stronger I felt weaker. What was missing?

A few days later God began to answer my question. I was having lunch with four friends from church. I told them about the clothing catalog. I shared that I hadn't looked at it, but that lust's power seemed to have increased. I had been struggling to guard my eyes in public. I kept thinking about the catalog. It felt like the lies of lust were still ringing in my ears and wearing me down.

Eric looked at me and with genuine care in his voice asked, "Are you memorizing any Scripture right now that can help you battle the lies of lust?"

Not really.

I had sort of dropped off lately. I could still recite Job 31:1: "I made a covenant with my eyes not to look lustfully at a girl." I could stumble my way through a few others. But I hadn't immersed myself in passages on the subject. I hadn't repeated them till their truth was coursing through my veins and fixed in my memory.

Suddenly it hit me how foolish I was being. I supposedly hated lust and its lies, but I wasn't fortifying my heart with the truth of God's Word. I'd gone into battle without my sword.

PICK UP YOUR SWORD

Throughout this book we've looked at many practical ways to avoid temptation. But we also have to know how to do battle when temptation has us in its grip. I want to teach you how to combat the lies of lust with the truth of God's Word. My goal is to do more than just suggest a few memory verses—I want to help you develop a *conviction* that Scripture is the only weapon that can successfully fight off lust.

Can you imagine how foolish it would be for a soldier to go into battle without his weapon or for him to let it fall into disrepair? As Christians, it's just as foolish for us to fight lust without the only offensive weapon God has given us.

Ephesians 6:17 calls the Word of God the "sword of the Spirit." Your Bible is no lifeless book. It has power. When you read it, speak it, and memorize it, the Holy Spirit uses it against sin like an offensive weapon. Hebrews 4:12 says:

> For the word of God is living and active. Sharper than any double-edged sword, it penetrates even to dividing soul and spirit, joints and marrow; it judges the thoughts and attitudes of the heart.

And 2 Timothy 3:16–17 states:

All Scripture is God-breathed and is useful for teaching, rebuking, correcting and training in righteousness, so that the man of God may be thoroughly equipped for every good work.

Scripture cuts through the confusion and hazy half-truths that our sin generates. It reveals our wrong desires. It rebukes our apathy. It corrects our selfish human thinking. It unmasks the deception of sin. It points us to God's goodness and faithfulness when we're tempted to forget. It trains us in righteousness. It counters the false promises of lust with God's true promises.

Since the day I was tempted by the catalog in the trash, I've learned that I can't reason with lust or argue against it with my own opinions. I can't put my fingers in my ears hoping to drown out its lies. And I'm definitely not going to last long if all I can answer is, "I'm not allowed to do that." I need an authority greater than my own. I need the very words of God. Hand-to-hand combat with lust doesn't work—I need the sword of the Spirit.

GETTING SPECIFIC

What are the specific lies your sinful desires tell you? Identify them and then go to God's Word and find passages that specifically address those lies. I've compiled the following list of Scriptures that I hope you find helpful. Don't rush through these. Consider the times you've been tempted by these lies; then let the truth of the Bible transform your perspective.

LIE

Lust is no big deal.

Truth: "For lust is a shameful sin, a crime that should be punished. It is a devastating fire that destroys to hell. It would wipe out everything I own" (Job 31:11–12, NLT).

LIE

A little sinful fantasizing won't hurt.

Truth: "To set the mind on the flesh is death, but to set the mind on the Spirit is life and peace" (Romans 8:6, ESV).

"Do not be deceived: God is not mocked, for whatever one sows, that will he also reap. For the one who sows to his own flesh will from the flesh reap corruption, but the one who sows to the Spirit will from the Spirit reap eternal life" (Galatians 6:7–8, ESV).

"But put on the Lord Jesus Christ, and make no provision for the flesh, to gratify its desires" (Romans 13:14, ESV).

LIE

Taking radical action against sin isn't necessary.

Truth: "If your right eye causes you to sin, gouge it out and throw it away. It is better for you to lose one part of your body than for your whole body to be thrown into hell. And if your right hand causes you to sin, cut it off and throw it away. It is better for you to lose one part of your body than for your whole body to go into hell" (Matthew 5:29–30).

"Flee the evil desires of youth, and pursue righteousness, faith, love and peace, along with those who call on the Lord out of a pure heart" (2 Timothy 2:22).

LIE

God won't mind a little compromise…

Truth: "Put to death, therefore, whatever belongs to your earthly nature: sexual immorality, impurity, lust, evil desires and greed, which is idolatry. Because of these, the wrath of God is coming" (Colossians 3:5–6).

"But among you there must not be even a hint of sexual immorality, or of any kind of impurity, or of greed, because these are improper for God's holy people" (Ephesians 5:3).

LIE

It's my body. I can do what I want with it.

Truth: "Flee from sexual immorality. All other sins a man commits are outside his body, but he who sins sexually sins against his own body. Do you not know that your body is a temple of the Holy Spirit, who is in you, whom you have received from God? You are not your own; you were bought at a price. Therefore honor God with your body" (1 Corinthians 6:18–20).

LIE

I can't control my sex drive.

Truth: "It is God's will that you should be sanctified: that you should avoid sexual immorality; that each of you should learn to control his own body in a way that is holy and honorable, not in passionate lust like the heathen, who do not know God; and that in this matter no one should wrong his brother or take advantage of him. The Lord will punish men for all such sins, as we have already told you and warned you" (1 Thessalonians 4:3–6).

LIE

Looking at a few pornographic pictures won't affect me.

Truth: "Do not lust in your heart after her beauty

or let her captivate you with her eyes, for the prostitute reduces you to a loaf of bread, and the adulteress preys upon your very life. Can a man scoop fire into his lap without his clothes being burned?" (Proverbs 6:25–27).

"I will set before my eyes no vile thing" (Psalm 101:3).

LIE

*I won't experience any consequences
for indulging in my lust.*

Truth: "So then, each of us will give an account of himself to God" (Romans 14:12).

"The Lord disciplines those he loves, and he punishes everyone he accepts as a son" (Hebrews 12:6).

"After desire has conceived, it gives birth to sin; and sin, when it is full-grown, gives birth to death" (James 1:15).

LIE

People get away with adultery.

Truth: "For the lips of an adulteress drip honey, and her speech is smoother than oil; but in the end she is bitter as gall, sharp as a double-edged sword. Her feet go down to death; her steps lead straight to the grave" (Proverbs 5:3–5).

"Keep to a path far from her, do not go near the door of her house, lest you give your best strength to others and your years to one who is cruel, lest strangers feast on your wealth and your toil enrich another man's house. At the end of your life you will groan, when your flesh and body are spent" (Proverbs 5:8–11).

LIE

God is keeping something good from me.

Truth: "Better is one day in your courts than a thousand elsewhere; I would rather be a door-keeper in the house of my God than dwell in the tents of the wicked. For the LORD God is a sun and shield; the LORD bestows favor and honor; no good thing does he withhold from those whose walk is blameless. O LORD Almighty, blessed is the man who trusts in you" (Psalm 84:10–12).

LIE

The pleasure lust promises is better and more real than God's pleasure.

Truth: "You have made known to me the path of life; you will fill me with joy in your presence, with eternal pleasures at your right hand" (Psalm 16:11).

LIE

Fulfilling my lust will satisfy me.

Truth: "I say to myself, 'The LORD is my portion; therefore I will wait for him.' The LORD is good to those whose hope is in him, to the one who seeks him; it is good to wait quietly for the salvation of the LORD" (Lamentations 3:24–26).

"The fear of the LORD leads to life, and whoever has it rests satisfied" (Proverbs 19:23, ESV).

LIE

Too much purity will keep me from seeing and enjoying beauty.

Truth: "Blessed are the pure in heart, for they will see God" (Matthew 5:8).

"For the LORD is righteous; he loves righteous deeds; the upright shall behold his face" (Psalm 11:7, ESV).

"Your eyes will behold the king in his beauty; they will see a land that stretches afar" (Isaiah 33:17, ESV).

Isn't Scripture incredible? Are you feeling its power as you read? Having the words of God engraved on your heart is the key to a life of purity. Psalm 119:9–11 says, "How can a young man keep his way pure? By living according to your word…. I have hidden your word in my heart that I might not sin against you."

Since lust can attack you at any time or place, you should be prepared wherever you are to fight back with Scripture. That's why I encourage you to commit the preceding list of verses to memory. Start by choosing one or two. Write them down on a card and place it where you'll see it—in your Bible, in your car, or on your computer. Review them several times a day. After a week pick a few more. Keep going till you have them all hidden in your heart.

In times of temptation, reciting several of these verses can be a wonderful deterrent to sin. I've found it helpful to pray them back to God. I use them to talk myself out of the deception of lust. Sometimes I even shout them. As I've done so, I've found renewed strength and faith to fight.

Power of a Promise

Part of sin is dissatisfaction with God. Lust's power comes from the promise it gives that something besides God can make us happy. What this means is that the only way to overcome the power of lust in our lives is by finding better promises. The key to holiness is satisfaction in God—faith that He is more to be desired than anything this world has to offer. We're not just turning away from lust; we're turning toward true satisfaction and joy in God.

We need to remember this in the midst of our struggle against lust. Sometimes fighting lust can appear to be the most illogical thing in the world. Every fiber of our bodies is telling us that giving in to lust will feel good and pleasurable—and we're supposed to fight this desire? I've learned that telling myself that whatever my lust is fixated on wouldn't really make me feel good doesn't work—because I know that, at least for little while, it would make me feel *very* good. I've learned that, as John Piper says, "The fire of lust's pleasures must be fought with the fire of God's pleasures."

So I don't deny that lust offers pleasure, but I glory in the promise of Psalm 16:11, which says, "You have made known to me the path of life; you will fill me with joy in your presence, with eternal pleasures at your right hand." The Inventor of all good pleasure has eternal pleasures waiting for you and me that we can't imagine or anticipate. All the experiences of pleasure we've known in this life are but faint echoes of what He has for us there.

Keep His Word always before you. Hide it in your heart. It will keep you close to Him and far from sin. Glory in God's promises. They're so much better than anything lust can offer.

chapter ten

Holiness Is
a Harvest

How Can I Sow to the Spirit?

If as you've reached the end
of this book, you're wondering where I shared the "secret"
to overcoming lust, you didn't miss it…. I don't have one.

I hope you're not disappointed. It *would* be nice to just
deal with lust once and for all and be done with it. But no
such quick fix exists. And I don't think we're supposed to
spend our time looking for it.

God's Word tells us how deep and lasting transformation takes place. It's not a secret. It's not even overly complicated. But it requires diligence and faith and daily dependence on His grace.

That's what this chapter is about. It's about how holiness happens in the lives of normal people. About how you and I can cooperate with God's Spirit and slowly but surely become more like Jesus Christ. The Bible offers a simple yet profound principle that I believe can give you faith for ongoing change:

> Do not be deceived: God cannot be mocked. A man reaps what he sows. The one who sows to please his sinful nature, from that nature will reap destruction; the one who sows to please the Spirit, from the Spirit will reap eternal life. Let us not become weary in doing good, for at the proper time we will reap a harvest if we do not give up. (Galatians 6:7–9)

The principle isn't exactly a revelation: "A man reaps what he sows." Any child knows that if you plant carrot seeds in a garden you will harvest carrots. You don't expect to get broccoli. We all understand that there's an unbreakable link between what we put into the ground and what we take out of it later.

The same principle is true in our spiritual lives. What you see in your spiritual life today is the direct result of what you've put in the soil of your life in days past. We can't get around this truth. There are no exceptions—our actions and choices can't be separated from specific consequences.

Do you know why some Christians make great strides in their walk with God while others are stagnant? Have you ever wondered if there is a godliness gene that some people are born with?

Of course there isn't. The difference between the person who grows in holiness and the one who doesn't is not a matter of personality, upbringing, or gifting; the difference is what each has planted into the soil of his or her heart and soul.

So holiness isn't a mysterious spiritual state that only an elite few can reach. It's more than an emotion, or a resolution, or an event. Holiness is a harvest.

WHERE WILL YOU SOW?

Where do we plant these seeds that will change our future for better or worse? Paul presents us with two fields. One represents the Spirit and a life lived to please and obey God. The other represents our sinful desires, or the "flesh."

Each of us can choose which field to plant seeds in. On any given day, or in any given moment, we can walk from one to the other, kneel down, and sow seeds in either one.

When it comes to the flesh, we do this by indulging in a lustful glance, a sinful fantasy, or a movie loaded with sexual innuendo. We might think of these acts as harmless little flecks of dirt we can just brush off every so often with no real damage done. But God is telling us here that our sinful thoughts and deeds are actually seeds that land in the soil of our flesh. They don't go away once they fall. They take root. They grow up. And eventually they become a great harvest of spiritual death.

John Stott writes, "Some Christians sow to the flesh every day and wonder why they do not reap holiness." This is why we've spent so much of this book talking about practical issues like the movies we watch and what we do with our eyes when we're in public. We want to stop sowing seeds to the flesh.

But that's not all we should do. Even more, we want to sow seeds in the field of righteousness. Growing in holiness is not about all the things you should avoid; it's about the wonderful things you can and should be doing instead.

We can't undo our past choices or escape their consequences, but starting today—starting *right now*—we can choose to sow to please the Spirit. Every choice, every thought, every conversation, every deed done to glorify God will lead to a harvest of eternal life!

SOWING TO THE SPIRIT

Sowing to please the Spirit involves all the big and small actions that seek to honor and exalt God in our lives.

We're sowing to the spirit when we...

- take time to read and study Scripture daily.
- gather with fellow believers in our local church to worship and be instructed by God's Word.
- serve in our local church.
- seek God in prayer.
- talk with a Christian friend about God's character and faithfulness.
- memorize passages of God's Word and meditate on His promises.
- read a Christian book that encourages us to love God more.
- listen to a Christian song that strengthens our faith.

All these activities and a hundred more are examples of sowing to the Spirit. But let me emphasize a few that are particularly important.

I believe that communing daily with God through reading His Word, through prayer, and through self-examination is among the most essential ways we can sow to the Spirit. There are many names for this. People call this a daily quiet time, devotions, or the spiritual disciplines.

In discussing the importance of private devotion, J. C. Ryle writes, "Here are the roots of true Christianity." He continues, "Wrong here, a man is wrong all the way through. Here is the whole reason why many professing Christians never seem to get on; they are careless and slovenly about their private prayers. They read their Bibles but little and with very little heartiness of spirit. They give themselves no time for self-inquiry and quiet thought about the state of their souls."

Do you want to grow in holiness? Do you want to see lust's power weaken in your life? Then make personal time with God the first priority of *every* day. Read your Bible with heartiness of spirit! Be diligent in prayer.

In the last two years I've experienced more strength to resist lust than I have at any other time in my life. Do you know why? I believe it's because God has helped me to make daily time in His Word a priority.

Ever since I was a teen, I've been inconsistent in the spiritual disciplines of Bible reading, prayer, and meditation. In the past I viewed it as something I was supposed to do—a chore that came with being a Christian. But God has helped me to see that it's not just part of my "Christian checklist." It's what I was created for.

The greatest privilege of my life isn't writing or speaking or being a pastor—it is relating to, communicating with, and knowing the Creator of the universe. Because Jesus died for my sins, I can draw near to God. In fact, He invites me to pray to Him, to know Him, to worship Him. There is nothing more wonderful! And there's nothing more important in our fight against lust. How can we expect to have strength to resist temptation and turn away from the lies of lust if we're not drawing strength from God's presence and having our hearts enlivened by His Spirit as we study His Word?

Do you want to experience lasting change? Do you want to grow in holiness? Sow seeds to the Spirit every day through private times with God. Pursue intimacy with Him.

PRACTICAL STEPS

How do you make this happen?

First, choose to make it the number one priority of your day. A priority pushes other things aside; a priority is unmoving; a priority lets other things bounce off it. I've found that it's best if I make time with God the first activity of my day. When this isn't possible, I do my best to reschedule for another time during the day. I even created a little system that helps me track my consistency on a monthly basis. I don't do this to be legalistic, but because it helps me see very clearly whether or not my time with God is truly a priority.

Second, have a plan for what you're going to do during your time with God. Decide what book of the Bible you're going to read through. If you're not used to studying the Bible and praying in private, here are several good books that can help you:

- *Spiritual Disciplines for the Christian Life* by Donald Whitney—This book provides lots of practical guidance on the disciplines of Bible study, prayer, meditation, fasting, journaling, and many others. Easy to read and inspiring.

- *Spiritual Reformation* by D. A. Carson—If you want to learn how to pray according to God's Word, you'll find this book very helpful. Dr. Carson uses the prayers of Paul as a guide for our own practice of prayer.

- *The Cross Centered Life* by C. J. Mahaney—You cannot successfully battle any sin apart from an awareness of God's grace. This small book will help you keep the gospel at the center of your faith. It will help you understand and love the Savior more.

- *Bible Doctrine* by Wayne Grudem—If you want to grow in your overall knowledge of God's Word, this book will guide you through what the Bible teaches about the major tenets of the Christian faith. It's good for new Christians as well as those who want to deepen their understanding of who God is.

- *Feminine Appeal* by Carolyn Mahaney—Each of the previous books are for men *and* women, but I wanted to recommend this book specifically for women. There is no better book I know of that can help women of all ages gain a biblical perspective on femininity and godliness. Carolyn is my pastor's wife and has mentored and discipled Shannon. Through the pages of this book, you too can benefit from her wisdom and insight.

You'll notice that none of these titles directly relate to sexual temptation. I don't think we should make overcoming lust our primary preoccupation—we need to make the gospel and God's glory our focus. We need to give ourselves to knowing Him, worshiping Him, and meeting with Him every day. The result will be the weakening of lust and a growing passion for godliness.

A Miracle in Progress

Has reading this book made you more aware of what needs to change in your life? If so, that's good. But also be aware that God is at work. Do you realize that? It is evidence of God's work in you that you would read a whole book about hating lust and loving holiness. Left to yourself, you wouldn't do that. That you made it this far is proof that God's Spirit is operating in your life.

And it's not over yet. You'll want to have a clear plan for following up in the areas God spoke to you about as you read this book. Here are few simple suggestions:

- Find an accountability partner in your church and read this book again together.
- Make sure the custom-tailored plan you created for fighting lust is posted somewhere where you'll see it often. And make sure to give a copy to your accountability partner.
- Start memorizing the Scripture verses from chapter 9 today.

- Create a plan for daily time with God. Choose what you'll study in God's Word and make it a daily habit. Make this the year that communion with God becomes the greatest priority of your life.

And don't give up! That's the encouragement of Galatians 6:9: "Let us not become weary in doing good, for at the proper time we will reap a harvest if we do not give up."

God knows that we can easily become discouraged. At times we want to throw our hands up and say, "Forget it!" There just seems to be too much to do and too far to go.

But don't become weary. As you sow to please the Spirit, a harvest of righteousness will begin to grow. It might not come up overnight, and at times you may feel like you're not changing at all. But you will be.

Remember that your hope for change is based in God's grace. It's because Jesus Christ died on the cross for your sins that you can stand justified before God and know that He will sanctify you day y. You can press toward God's standard of *not even a hint* of sexual immorality in the unshakable confidence that through faith in Christ you stand before God with not even a hint of guilt.

Because of Jesus Christ, we can have victory over lust. Sometimes we want a victory that means no more struggle.

God calls us to trust Him in the struggle against lust, to persevere and so prove the reality of the victory accomplished by His Son. John Piper calls it the "persevering fight."

Remember, God doesn't call you to sacrifice as an end in itself. He calls you through it. On the other side of sacrifice is unspeakable beauty and indescribable joy. It's not easy, but it's worth every minute.

So welcome to the persevering fight. Welcome to the mystery of dying to yourself and finding real life. Welcome to the pleasure and freedom of holiness.

Purity Download

Seven Tips for Fighting Internet Porn

by Joshua Harris

he Internet is a wonderful tool. We can use it to work, to study, to play, even to share the gospel with people in other parts of the world. But if you and I aren't careful, it can become a door to great sin and spiritual ruin. Christian men and women, church leaders included, have fallen prey to the temptations of lust on-line. Whether it's illicit relationships in chat rooms, immoral blog content, or pornographic sites, the invitation to sin is especially dangerous because the Internet is so accessible and what we see and do there is so easily hidden from others. But God sees all our sin. And impurity of any kind will always lead to heartache and regret. Whether or not this is a current area of temptation for you, the following seven tips will equip you to honor God on-line.

1. IDENTIFY WHAT'S LEADING UP TO LUSTFUL INDULGENCE ON THE INTERNET.

For most people, sin on-line is preceded by compromise in areas such as their fantasies, television viewing, or reading material. It might seem like sexual sin on-line "comes out of nowhere," but it's really something we build up to through disobedience in other areas. Prayerfully consider where you can be fighting the little battles more diligently so you can avoid the big ones.

2. RESOLVE THAT NO TECHNOLOGICAL CONVENIENCE IS WORTH SINNING AGAINST GOD.

Most people have to use the Internet for school or work. But we should never place the convenience of technology above God's commands for holiness. If you've struggled with Internet porn or impurity of any kind, be willing to take radical action. Maybe that means no Internet access at your home for a season. Or not having high-speed access. Or staying away from chat rooms or specific kinds of surfing, period. It could mean going on-line only when you're with other people. My dad has only one computer in his house with a web browser, and that computer is in the middle of the living room. But that's not all…my mom is the only one with the password to get onto it!

Inconvenient? Incredibly so! But he's more concerned with protecting himself and my younger brothers than with convenience.

3. EXAMINE YOUR MIND-SET WHEN BROWSING AND THE AMOUNT OF TIME SPENT ON-LINE.

Susan found herself increasingly going on-line when she was feeling lonely or depressed. Not surprisingly, it wasn't long before she got involved in visiting sites that led her into sin. If Internet use has become a mindless entertainment activity, where your brain goes into neutral and your defenses are down, you're in dangerous territory. You might not be struggling with Internet impurity right now, but there's a good chance that your behavior and mind-set will lead you there soon. Go on-line with a purpose. And don't spend tons of time browsing aimlessly. Cutting back so that the time you spend on-line is focused and has a point will significantly cut back on the temptation to slip into the darker corners of the Web.

4. HAVE AN ACCOUNTABILITY PARTNER THAT CONSISTENTLY ASKS ABOUT YOUR INTERNET ACTIVITY.

Even if you don't have a history of struggling with Internet porn, you need a friend who regularly asks how you're doing in this area. Find someone you trust and respect of the same gender who will put the question to you straight—and wait for your answer. Then get a commitment from him or her to put you on the spot regularly.

5. REDEFINE "OVER THE LINE" (IT'S NOT THE EDGE OF THE CLIFF)

Jared had been struggling with temptation to look at on-line porn for a week. He'd been testing his resolve by visiting somewhat questionable sites, and the urge to indulge kept growing. Unfortunately, he didn't tell his accountability partner what was happening. Instead he battled in secret. A week later, after he "really messed up" and spent two hours browsing porn sites, he finally called his accountability partner.

Do you see the problem? Jared's definition of "over the line" when it comes to sin is right at the edge of the cliff. That means when he finally confesses, he's already fallen.

When it comes to accountability, I think it's important to back up our definition of messing up on-line. We need to involve others much earlier in the process of temptation. So confess when you're dabbling with somewhat questionable sites (or okay sites with provocative ads or other content). Share when you're spending too much time on-line. Make these behaviors your definition of crossing the line so your friends can pray for you and challenge you long before you slip off the edge of temptation into sin. I like what Thomas Watson once wrote: "A godly man will not go as far as he may, lest he go further than he should."

6. USE WEBSITE FILTERS, BLOCKERS, AND ACCOUNTABILITY SOFTWARE AS A FINAL LINE OF DEFENSE, NOT THE FIRST.

Programs that e-mail a list of all the websites you visit or block bad content are a wonderful tool. But they can't replace a heart that truly hates sin and desires to please God. Utilize them after you've taken a look at your heart and examined the lies you tell yourself in the process of temptation. Do the work of digging into God's Word, meditating on Scripture, making yourself accountable, and other steps listed above. Otherwise you're likely to find yourself looking for ways and times to get around the technological fence you've put in place. Instead, get your heart convictions in the right place; then your blocking and accountability software can serve to support your commitments.

7. FIGHT THIS SIN THE HARDEST WHEN YOU'RE FEELING STRONG.

Many people experience a level of "victory" over Internet porn for a season—only to be lulled into a false sense of security and fall again. If you're experiencing a time of relative freedom from impure behavior on-line, that's good…but don't stop watching this part of your life carefully. It's when you're feeling strong that you should fight the hardest. In other words, kick sin when it's down. You don't have to fight like a gentleman here. Redouble your grace-motivated efforts. Keep "backing up" your definition of on-line compromise. Memorize Scripture. Pray for God's power. By doing so you'll weaken the power of this sin in your life even more.

The Path of Repentance

by John Loftness

STEP 1: PRAY

- Establish your dependence on God by praying for the Holy Spirit's help in this process.

STEP 2: IDENTIFY THE SIN

- Define its practice in biblical terms.
- Define your heart's motive for the sin in biblical terms.
- Define the lie—the false belief—that created this motive and its acts.

STEP 3: EMBRACE THE GOSPEL

- Meditate on how your sin offends God. Cultivate sorrow.
- Meditate on the fact that God sent Jesus to die in your place to overcome the offense this sin created.
- Pray. Admit your sin to God and ask Him to forgive you and to account this sin to Jesus' death on your behalf.

STEP 4: TAKE STEPS TO STOP

- Collect on paper what the Bible says about your sin, its consequences, your forgiveness in Christ, and the Spirit's power at work in you to change. Memorize the most helpful passages.
- Purpose to change your thinking and your behavior.
- Purpose to change behavior that increases temptation:
  - Places you go
  - People with whom you interact
  - Things you look at or listen to
  - Words you say
  - Confess your sin to those you've offended and seek their forgiveness. Make restitution if necessary.

STEP 5: REPLACE YOUR SIN WITH RIGHTEOUSNESS

- "Put on Christ." If you're a Christian, you are joined to Jesus Christ. His Spirit dwells within you. You can think and act as He does!

- Identify thoughts you can think or actions you can take to replace:
  - The lie with truth
  - The sinful motive with a true motive for something else that pleases God
  - Sinful behavior with righteous behavior

STEP 6: SEEK FELLOWSHIP AS A MEANS OF GRACE

- If you haven't already, inform godly friends or a pastor of your sin and the process you are engaging in to change.
- Ask for their evaluation of the conclusions you've drawn, and adjust where needed.
- Make yourself accountable to walk along the specific path you've outlined above.

STEP 7: REVIEW

- Steps 1–5 daily.
- Step 6 for regular accountability.

Acknowledgments

A special thanks…

To Doug Gabbert and Kevin Marks, who helped me
determine what book I should write next, fought for a
good title, and diligently supported me throughout the
project.

To Corby Megorden, the administrator at Covenant
Life Church, who bore the brunt of my absence at the
office. His faithfulness made it possible for me to focus
fully on writing. To the rest of my fellow pastors who support my writing and prayed for me each Tuesday.

To Cara Nalle, my research assistant, who conducted
all the interviews with women and gave me feedback on
how to make the book more helpful to women.

To my editors David and Heather Kopp. This husband
and wife team guided me through the seemingly impossible

182 SEX IS NOT THE PROBLEM (LUST IS)

task of writing a book in four months. They challenged me, argued with me, encouraged me, and cheered me on as I found my voice. In many moments of confusion, it was Heather's willingness to wrestle with my tangled drafts that brought clarity. To Jennifer Gott, who did the line edit.

To C. J. Mahaney, my friend, pastor, and boss, who assigned me to speak on this subject and suggested that I turn the message into a book the minute I was done speaking. He gave me the time off to write, read every chapter, and provided feedback, then relentlessly encouraged me. And thanks for the Titanium PowerBook.

To Shannon, my dearest friend and partner. I cannot honor her enough. I'm able to write because she joyfully embraces her calling as a wife and mother. Besides all the exhausting duties of caring for our two kids and managing a home, she read chapters to me out loud so I could hear what they sounded like, put up with my "writing zombie" moments, and sang "Happy Book Day" to me when I finished. All my passion is for you, my love.

To my Lord and Savior, Jesus Christ. Thank You for saving me. This book is because of You and for You.

Notes

PREFACE
   Jerry Bridges—Jerry Bridges, *The Discipline of Grace* (Colorado Springs, Colo.: NavPress, 1994).

CHAPTER 1
   John Piper—John Piper, *Future Grace* (Sisters, OR: Multnomah, 1995), 336.

CHAPTER 2
   C. S. Lewis—C. S. Lewis, *Mere Christianity* (New York: Macmillan, 1952), 76.

CHAPTER 3
   The story of Raynald III was taken from Thomas Costain's *The Three Edwards*, retold in *Illustrations for Preaching and Teaching*, ed. Craig Brian Larson (Grand Rapids, MI: Baker Books, 1993), 229.
   John Owen—John Owen, *Sin & Temptation*, ed. James M.

Houston (Minneapolis, MN: Bethany, 1996), 153.

C. J. Mahaney—C. J. Mahaney, *The Cross Centered Life* (Sisters, OR: Multnomah, 2002), 30–2.

John Stott—John R. W. Stott, *The Message of Galatians* (Downers Grove, IL: InterVarsity Press, 1968), 143.

"Before the Throne of God"—© 1997 PDI Worship, words and music by Charitie Lees Bancroft and Vikki Cook.

John Stott—Stott, *The Message of Galatians,* 143.

CHAPTER 4

Richard Baxter—Richard Baxter, "Directions for Hating Sin," *Fire and Ice,* www.puritansermons.com/baxter/baxter16.htm (accessed 21 April 2003).

CHAPTER 5

Dr. Al Mohler—Dr. Al Mohler shared his statement on men giving themselves to pornography and women committing pornography in a conversation with the author.

CHAPTER 6

Jeffrey Black—Jeffrey Black, *Sexual Sin: Combating the Drifting and Cheating* (Phillipsburg, NJ: P&R Publishing, 2003), 6–7. This booklet can be ordered by contacting Resources for Changing Lives, 1803 E. Willow Grove Ave., Glenside, PA 19038 or call (800) 318-2186.

CHAPTER 7

Letter from Mrs. Wesley—Wesley, from a letter to her son John, June 1725. The General Commission on Archives and History, The United Methodist Church, http://www.gcah.org/COUMH/VoiceSWesley.htm (accessed 24 April 2003).

Joel Belz—Joel Belz, Editorial, *World,* 28 September 1996, 5.
Ibid.

Wayne Wilson—Wayne Wilson, *Worldly Amusements: Restoring the Lordship of Christ to Our Entertainment Choices* (Enumclaw, WA: Winepress Publishing, 1999), 19–20.

CHAPTER 8

Alan Medinger—Alan Medinger, as quoted in the *Journal of Biblical Counseling* 13, no. 3 (Spring 1995), 54–5. For subscription information, call (215) 884-7676 or visit www.ccef.org.

CHAPTER 9

The idea of battling the lies of lust with the true promises of God's Word was inspired by John Piper and his book *Future Grace.*

John Piper—Piper, *Future Grace,* 336.

CHAPTER 10

The title of this chapter was inspired by John Stott.

John Stott—Stott, *The Message of Galatians*, 170.

J. C. Ryle—J. C. Ryle, *Holiness* (Grange Close, Darlington: Evangelical Press, 1999), 89.

John Piper—Piper, *Future Grace,* 332.

About the Author

Joshua Harris is the lead pastor of Covenant Life Church in Gaithersburg, Maryland. A gifted speaker with a passion for making theological truth easy to understand, Joshua is perhaps best known for his runaway bestseller, *I Kissed Dating Goodbye,* which he wrote at the age of twenty-one. His later books include *Boy Meets Girl, Not Even a Hint,* and *Why Church Matters.* He and his wife, Shannon, have three children.

www.joshharris.com
twitter.com/harrisjosh
www.facebook.com/joshharris.fanpage

Ready to Rethink Dating?

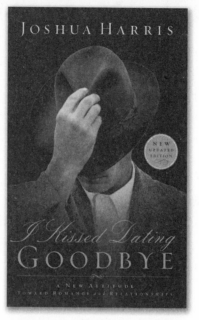

Going out? Been dumped? Waiting for a call that doesn't come? Have you tasted pain in dating, drifting through one romance or possibly several of them? Ever wondered, *Isn't there a better way?*

I Kissed Dating Goodbye shows what it means to entrust your love life to God. Joshua Harris shares his story of giving up dating and discovering that God has something even better—a life of sincere love, true purity, and purposeful singleness.

Are You Ready for Romance with Purpose?

If you're fed up with self-centered relationships that end in disillusionment, it's time to rethink romance. Finding the loving, committed relationship you want shouldn't mean throwing away your hopes, your integrity, or your heart. As old-fashioned as it might sound, courtship is what modern-day relationships desperately need. Think of it as romance chaperoned by wisdom, cared for by community, and directed by God's Word. Learn how courtship can keep God, the Author of romance, at the center of your relationship.

Are You Dating the Church?

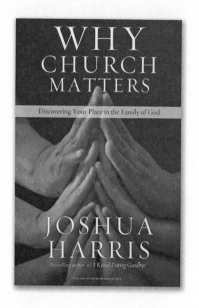

We are a generation of consumers, independent and critical. We attend church, but we don't want to settle down and truly invest ourselves. We're not into commitment—we only want to date the church. Is this what God wants for us?

Why Church Matters reminds us that faith was never meant to be a solo pursuit. The church is the place where God grows us, encourages us, and uses us best. Loving Jesus Christ involves a passionate commitment to His church—around the world and down the street. We can't be apathetic. It's time to fall in love with the family of God.

REDISCOVER
the relevance and power
of Christian truth in your life

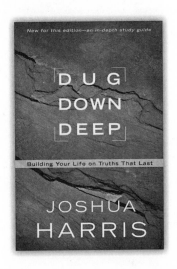

With humor and engaging reflections on Christian beliefs, Harris shows that orthodoxy isn't just for scholars—it is for anyone who longs to know the living Jesus Christ. Whether you are just exploring Christianity or you are a veteran believer finding yourself overly familiar and cold-hearted, *Dug Down Deep* will help you rediscover the timeless truths of Scripture.

"Theology matters because if we get it wrong then our whole life will be wrong."
– Joshua Harris